FROM
COLLEGE
STRESS ━━━━▶ TO
SUCCESS

Save time, simplify studying and
ace your college experience

BRAD SMITH

CONTENTS

Section 2: The Legwork

INTRODUCTION

College was the most memorable time of my life, and it should be for you, too. The memories, friends, and growth I experienced are unforgettable. On top of that, I received a diploma, which set me up for professional success.

Can it be stressful and challenging? You bet. You may be thinking, *How can I enjoy college if my stress and anxiety levels are through the roof?* That's where I want to help you. In knowing the importance of academic performance yet desiring an active social life, I've experienced that dilemma and fear. It overwhelmed me with anxiety. With all my struggles, I'm here to say there's a way to have it all. You're spending a lot of money to receive that diploma. You better make that little piece of paper worth it.

College is an adventure. I'm sure you've already asked all the college graduates you know about how college is and what to expect. People won't hesitate to give you plenty of advice and expectations. Nevertheless, you'll never understand college until you experience it yourself. Every college experience is unique and new to each individual. The atmosphere's different in so many ways. It's a significant change from your typical day-to-day experiences while you were in high school. No matter the size of your town or school, you grew up in what I like to call the "high school bubble."

I call it a bubble because most teenagers are isolated from other aspects of the world. They're accustomed to their high school environment. You're familiar with and used to your high school and hometown and the culture and traditions they bring. You ran into the same people, saw the same things, shared the same beliefs.

College is an opportunity to pop this bubble. The experience gathers people from all over the world and brings them into one place that blends everything. The differences among the people, places, and lifestyles will open your perspective. It broadens you as an individual.

I grew up and attended school in a small suburban city, surrounded by farmland on one side and industrial complexes on the other. In other words, one side of town was cornfields, while the other was steel mills as far as the eye can see.

My high school lacked ethnic diversity. It consisted of around 900-1,000 students, and approximately 93% were White/Caucasian. The only people I interacted with were kids of the same race as me who also grew up in this same environment. We all had similar backgrounds and a common enemy of our high school sports rival. The most significant form of diversity in our school was what sports teams you cheered for. You were either a Cleveland sports fan or a Pittsburgh sports fan. All this was my high school bubble.

The bubble popped when I attended college. It contained people from every different race, from all over the world. The only thing I felt I had in common with anyone at the university was that we were attending the same college. Every day was an eye-opening experience for me. My life now consists of different outlooks and new viewpoints. I had never considered these before. You're currently or soon will be experiencing this new environment, and it's exciting. The cherry on top of it all is that you're also on your own.

When you're in college, you're independent. You should be right around that 18-year-old mark. It doesn't matter what your inner self tells you because, in the eyes of the government, you're officially an adult. When you enrolled in college, it's through your name, not your parents. Any issues, problems, or information about college will have to go through you. If you take out student loans, they have to be in your name. If you're living on campus, it's a good possibility that this is the first time living on your own. You're the star of the show now with responsibilities at an all-time high. You're in charge, in the driver's seat.

Welcome to adulthood. You're responsible for yourself and all the actions you take. The reins are free. You're in charge of your day-to-day schedule: when you want to take classes, when you want to eat, who you want to see, when you want to go to bed, and when to study. Anything and everything dealing with your life is in your hands and your control with brand new places and environments. At first, this may feel freeing and amazing. You'll then start realizing that you may need to take a step back or you'll begin to lose control. Most, if not all, of your previous support groups are removed from you. Your success and well-being is 100% dependent on yourself. You have a lot to take in and a lot to balance in that first year of college. It can be overwhelming at times. With this realization, fear, doubt, and anxiety may start to kick in and bog you down.

All this new responsibility and pressure can make college stressful. You now have to figure out everything for yourself, interact with new people, and attend and pass college-level courses. Every action you do may affect your future outside of college. This pressure and stress could have catastrophic consequences for you and your health. It needs to be monitored and kept in check.

My first semester of college was a whirlwind. It was my first time living by myself with an assigned random roommate. This roommate had the complete opposite background as me, and we had nothing in common. I had scheduled 16 credit hours and was on the baseball team for the university. All my close friends from high school went to different colleges, so I was alone. I had the perception of myself as a tiny minnow in the middle of an immense ocean.

Class homework and assignments began to pile up. Practice and workout times became more frequent and more prolonged. I had to understand how to cook, clean, do laundry, etc. I had to figure out how to make new friends and acquaintances. All on top of trying to get good grades in my classes. I thought to myself, *How can I do this? Can I even do this?*

Most of those fears began to fade as I got more comfortable in this new environment. Yet the stress of getting good grades never passed. Every so often, a professor would give a short lecture that had nothing to do with actual class material. They would talk about the time they expect you to spend outside of the classroom reading and studying if you want to be successful in their classes. The amount of time recommended demoralized me. Even though I wanted to succeed in everything, my hopes in achieving this dwindled. My goal for college was to make new friends, have fun, and graduate with a top tier GPA. After listening to my professors, though, that was becoming less likely.

What's the point of college? The answer may seem easy, but it has evolved and became somewhat convoluted over the years. Throughout my years in school, the most common response I heard was that college is what they thought their next step should be. They're so accustomed to the education system; college comes after high school. College is the next steppingstone. They had no idea of what they wanted their future to be after education.

Anyone going to college should have a basic understanding of their life projection, the career they want to have, nothing too specific, but a general idea of what field they want to specialize in. Do you want a career in business, education, communication, health, or human services? The specific major doesn't have to come right away. Sticking to a similar field will make it easier if you need to switch your particular major. You also won't waste too much time and money if you do it this way. Getting a good-paying job after graduation is what most people think college is all about. Don't get me wrong; this is important and should be the main focus of all students. Still, it shouldn't be the only focus.

College isn't all about getting a good paying job. Another, unforeseen benefit is a byproduct of college. College is a time when you discover yourself. You're independent, possibly for the first time, in a new environment with new people, and exposed to different viewpoints and ideas. You'll realize different outlooks on life and enlightening new topics. The opportunities for meeting new people and growing countless relationships are endless. This is when people usually make that initial transition from adolescence to adulthood.

Many skills can be developed and sharpened throughout your time in college such as people skills, networking, charisma, the ability to small talk, and approachability. You will have so many opportunities to improve these skills. These all contribute to future success and happiness after college. College is more than academics. Facebook conducted a survey analyzing marriage statistics. The study showed that 28% of married graduates attended the same college as their spouse.[1] I'm lucky enough to be a part of those statistics.

I met my wife at a house party when I was a sophomore. I was hesitant to even go to this party. It was only two weeks before our baseball season kicked off. Despite this, I convinced myself that I needed to be more social. I ended up going to this party at an on-campus apartment. I sat on the couch, mingling with someone I knew. After a couple of minutes, the conversation was getting stale. I then scanned my eyes through the room. I saw this girl sitting at the kitchen counter singing the "Cup Song" from the movie, *Pitch Perfect*. While she sang, she was doing the whole routine with these red solo cups. Her infectious smile, contagious laughter, and beautiful singing voice captivated me. I went over, sat down, and asked if she could show me how to do the cup routine. I met up with her at a couple of parties the following weeks, and a couple of months later, I asked her on our first real date. The rest was history. College is more than just getting a degree. All opportunities college presents should be taken advantage of.

Opportunities are endless in college. Countless clubs and organizations are available to college students. Some are more traditional that deal with politics, theater, and sports, and others are unique. My school had some far-out clubs. Believe it or not, we had a squirrel watching club, a Nerf gun war club, Frisbee golf club, movie club, and the list goes on. Get involved in as much as you can. If you think an organization or club will bring you happiness or growth, join it. College is a time for self-discovery, growth, and freedom. The overarching theme in all this is to find things that you enjoy and have fun doing. Get involved.

In the second semester of my freshman year, I was sitting on a charter bus headed home from a baseball trip. A pit began to form in my stomach, knowing I had two tests the next day that I had barely prepared for. The uneasiness in my stomach began to intensify, and my heart started pounding. My breath rate increased. Self-doubt started to creep in my mind. How am I supposed to study for two tests in an 8-hour bus ride? I only have a small night light, no table, my neck hurts, and getting carsick. I started to get a slight panic attack. I wanted to do it all and succeed in my classes, yet I didn't know how.

I started by reading as many class notes and textbook chapters as I could for the next eight hours. While I was intensely studying, jealousy began to form. I heard all my teammates talking, laughing, and playing games. I took a deep sigh, put in my headphones and kept on studying for the remainder of the bus ride.

I ended up taking the tests the next day, tired and exhausted. After a couple of days, the results of the tests came back. I received an average grade on both tests. I was frustrated. I missed out on the fun times my teammates were having on the bus.

On top of that, I spent eight-plus hours studying getting carsick. There had to be a quicker way that also would get me better grades. I needed a process that I could follow or a set of choices that I could make that would help me achieve these goals. I didn't want to have any more panic attacks. I wanted to feel confident. I needed something that would help me be more prepared and create more free time.

I started to reflect on the most crucial aspect of studying. What's the most significant waste of time during studying? Reflecting on both of these questions, I realized an answer. I needed to understand the main points the professor taught during class. Also, coupling those points with more information that's in the textbook. I also realized the most significant waste of time was reading the textbook page by page, word for word. Also, going through many pages of random notes and scanning through many handouts wasted time. As I pondered this predicament, a light bulb went off. I began to start a new strategy: Put all the information I needed for a test in one location, summarized, organized, and condensed. After many weeks of constant improvement upon this idea, I developed a method of studying that saved me tons of time. I also saw definite progress in my test performances and final grades.

This book will break down this method of studying. The goal is to save time through efficient studying. With that time saved, you can succeed in every aspect of college. This method got me to experience college to the fullest. I never received a grade lower than an A. I was part of a championship-winning division 1 baseball program. I made great friends and created many new fulfilling relationships. College created and opened so many opportunities in my life. I experienced growth throughout my four years of college. The method made my future more significant and brighter.

I accredit all this success to the methods explained in this book. If you adopt the practices and suggestions in this book, improvements will come. Your grades will improve, your happiness will increase, and your future will be bright. Waiting isn't an option. College only gets harder as you get older. There's no time like today. The earlier you instill these practices, the more benefit you'll receive from them. Time becomes more precious as you get closer to graduating. More items will be on your plate, and the more difficult the coursework will be. There will be suggestions, strategies, and tactics presented in this book. Take your time, read, and adopt. Your success depends on it.

This book has two main sections: The groundwork and the legwork. The groundwork is the foundation that needs to be in place and installed in your daily life. They're principles that establish excellence for successful people. Groundwork is the setup to make the new studying methods and processes most effective. This foundation is the only way to maximize your potential in college. The legwork is the new studying process. These practices will vastly improve retention while limiting the time spent. Please take the time to absorb the information in this book. They're the tried and true methods developed through personal experiences. My failures and my successes paved these roads. Congratulations, because you just took the first step to a successful college career. Enjoy.

SECTION 1

THE GROUNDWORK

The groundwork is usually overlooked, especially by young adults. Most think all they need is a hack for study to get good grades in college. But the proper mindset and the pieces you have to put in place give you better results. The best part about establishing this groundwork is that it takes minimal effort. Don't confuse its simplicity with futility. It's paramount in achieving greatness and requires focus and deliberate execution.

The groundwork will first cover the two common myths deterring college student triumph, then eliminating those myths from your mind. Then the groundwork is divided into three subsections: Mindset, Environment, and Work Ethic. These three subsections will layout the foundation for your inevitable success.

I learned from the early stages in my life, what it takes to be successful. I spent most of my childhood playing travel baseball. Travel baseball was a high demand, high intensity, year-long commitment. Our goal was nothing short of greatness, and our travel team showed it. A group of my friends started a travel baseball team at the age of eight years old. We wanted to play more than the little league season, so we formed a team. It wasn't long before we realized that the team we had assembled was something special. We kept winning and winning and winning. We won all three tournaments that we signed up for and knew we couldn't stop there. We had to keep going. This travel team transitioned into the following year as nine-year-old kids. We expanded our talent by adding a couple more kids from the local area. We started the year where we left off, winning. We won over 90% of all our games and were invited to play in the USSSA World Series!

We were ecstatic when we found out that we were going to the World Series! Yet, there was one small problem: we only had 12 kids on our team. Most of the tournaments we played in that year were only a couple of games played over five days. The games were spaced enough that we didn't need that many players to win. That's why we only carried 12 players. Out of those 12 players, five were in our pitching rotation. To grow the number of pitchers we had on our team, a couple of players would pitch when we had blowout victories. Our coach then could decide to make them a pitcher for the long term.

That's where I came in. I was our team's primary third baseman and also played a little outfield, so I had a strong arm. I came in to pitch in those blowouts. I showed that I had the potential to be a good pitcher; however, I was unpredictable, wild. I had no idea of the proper pitching mechanics or how to throw strikes consistently. I liked pitching and wanted to get better, so I started taking lessons. I had a desire to improve my pitching abilities. My goal was to become one of our team's top pitchers so that I could contribute more to my team.

During our 9-year-old season, five pitchers were all that we needed to succeed. A pitcher would throw one game, and after three days' rest, he was up throwing again. The problem was that the world series was double elimination. We had to play anywhere from 7 to 9 games over five days if we wanted to win. We recognized that we had a problem. We didn't have the pitching to play that many games in that short of time. To play the least amount of games, we had to win out. We needed to stay out of the loser's bracket at all costs. The loser's bracket is where you play all the extra games. We knew what we had to do to avoid using any of our inexperienced reserve pitchers.

The day before we left, we had one last practice as a tune-up. Before we all left, my coach pulled me off to the side. He told me that I was the first reserve pitcher outside of our regular rotation, and I had to be ready to pitch if needed. I remember freezing up, and doubt started to creep into my mind. *I'm not prepared to throw in a world series*, I thought. Then I altered my thought process and began to doubt myself. Our pitchers were way too good, and they won't need me to pitch, there will be nothing to worry about. We're going to win out!

We steamrolled through all three teams in the pool-play section of the tournament. The dominance in pool-play established us as a top seed going into bracket play. We then won the first two games in bracket play. At this point, we were in the semifinals and could see our pathway to victory. We huddled up as a team and started conversing and pumping each other up for this next game. Every kid on our team tried to come with either a motivational saying or a short speech to get everyone excited. Then we realized that we had a big problem; we had no available pitchers for this game.

The pitcher who was supposed to pitch had arm pain and wasn't ready to perform for this game. Right when we figured that out, the head coach called me to come over to him. I staggered over, eyes wide. He told me I would be starting pitching in this game and to be ready to go. He went on explaining to me that if we won this game, we would be in the championship with our ace pitcher, a for-sure win. He finished up the conversation by telling me that he had faith in me and knew I could do it. As he walked away, I froze, and all the doubt in the world started to creep into my mind. How could I pitch in the semifinals of the world series? Our success as a team rides on my shoulders.

Warming up before the game, I kept on thinking I'm not ready for this. I'm not as good as our other pitchers. I'm wild, and I don't even have a good changeup. I'm not ready for this. After around 30 min of this negative self-talk, I realized that I was going to pitch no matter what. I tried to snap myself out of this downward spiral and pump myself up. It was too late. The negative emotions and fear had overcome me, and I couldn't escape from it. Walking out to the mound, I felt the weight of the moment on my shoulders. I knew all my teammates' hopes and dreams for this season were up to me to fulfill. I took a deep breath and stepped on the mound and started pitching.

The first inning didn't go too badly. I had only given up one run. Not great, but manageable. The second inning, I gave up another run. On the bright side, we scored one as well. At this moment, our team was losing 2-1 in the top of the third. That's when all hell broke loose.

I stepped on the mound for the third time and started to throw. The next thing I remember was the scoreboard, and it said "6 -1", with a big bold number 5 in the top of the 3rd column. Tears started forming in my eyes, and everything turned blurry. I knew we had already lost, and it was all my fault. I threw one more pitch. The batter hit a slow ground ball right back up the middle. This ground ball should have been a piece of cake, but all the tears in my eyes made it so I couldn't see the ball. I missed that easy ground ball and another run scored.

It was then, our coach came in and pulled me from the game. I sat on the bench and stared at the ground for the next couple innings realizing that I had blown it for my team. I told myself I would never pitch again, that I was terrible, and didn't have the "stuff" to be a good pitcher.

This experience caused me never to want to get on another pitcher's mound again. I wanted to give up on pitching and focus on other areas of baseball. Even though I thought this, my parents still thought I could be a great pitcher and kept pushing me to take lessons.

Throughout the next couple of months, I took many painstaking pitching lessons. To my disbelief, I started to see improvement. An optimistic light began to form in my perception. Maybe I could be a decent pitcher!

Months turned into years of constant lessons. Even though I was still not a regular pitcher for my travel team, I was taking lessons. It wasn't until I was 15 years old that I started to get consistent pitching appearances in games. At 15, I knew I was a good pitcher and could dominate when I was on the mound. It took six years to get to this point after the traumatizing game that demoralized my psyche.

Now I had confidence. My pitching reflected that, and I had a prosperous pitching career in high school. I also played exceptionally in my summer travel league. By the end of my senior year, I had obtained interest from many Division 1 schools to be a pitcher. Ultimately receiving two scholarship offers from two of those division 1 baseball programs. I was able to have my college education paid for because of my ability as a pitcher.

I credit the success in my baseball career to three significant aspects of my life. First, I had a mindset change. When I first started pitching, I had doubts and was cynical about my ability to be a pitcher. Once I began to think differently, focused on the positives, and had a purpose, I knew I could do it. Everything changed for the better.

The next reason was that I had an excellent support team with my family and friends. They were all role models who pushed me to be better and were always there for me. Finally, I put in the work. I worked hard on all the aspects of great pitchers, including my pitching mechanics, arm strength, control, and maintenance. To get that baseball scholarship, I put in the time and work. The hours I spent practicing and getting better are countless. Hard work is a necessity.

Your mindset, surrounding environment, and work ethic are the keys to success. We'll be diving deep into each one of these topics in the following chapters. Before we do that, it's essential to discuss the common myths deterring your success in college.

ELIMINATING THE MYTHS OF COLLEGE SUCCESS

Myth #1: I don't have the genetics to get good grades

The first myth is essentially the go-to excuse for people who give up. It's an easy out. It's a way to convince yourself that you have no shot at getting good grades even if you try. It's also a way for people to belittle the work that other colleagues have done—discrediting the time that they put in to obtain higher grades.

Most people believe that to achieve success in academics, you have to be a gifted intellectual. Two fallacies connected to this belief need to be discussed.

1. Genetics determines intelligence is FALSE. It can be altered throughout your life by the actions and choices you make.
2. Intelligence is the only factor in achieving academic success is FALSE. More factors come into play, especially the older you get.

First, let's break down what intelligence is. Intelligence is something that helps you plan, problem solve, and quickly learn. It also enables you to think on your feet and make decisions. Ultimately, intelligence helps you survive this fast-moving world. Over the last decade, genome-wide association studies (GWAS) have conducted many investigations. Their focus was on human traits and their relation to the whole "nature vs. nurture" debate.

Intelligence studies yielded mostly non-replicable results. These findings show that intelligence is a highly polygenic trait, meaning that many different genes would exert extremely small, if any, influence. Also, most of these polygenic traits exert influence at various stages of development.[2] In other words, there's no such thing as a single "Intelligence or IQ Gene." It doesn't exist. Not only do the genes that affect intelligence have a small impact, but they also impact at different moments throughout life.

Intelligence isn't entirely defined by genetics. It has strong environmental determinants as well. The brain is malleable and is affected by daily experiences and education. Therefore, our cognitive functions or how we process information can also be altered, changed, and improved. You have to be aware of outside contributors. How were you raised? What's your current work ethic? Are you maintaining robust mental health? Also, be mindful of any other life actions and daily experiences. They all affect our brains and learning capabilities.

People try to quantify intelligence through a calculated number called IQ, generated through a test meant to capture and measure a person's reasoning ability. In theory, the higher the IQ score, the more intelligent you're supposed to be. Studies show that higher IQ scores have a positive influence on academic success. However, it's not an absolute correlation.

The correlations between academic success and IQ scores decrease as you progress. Studies have shown that the correlation in elementary students is around 0.7. That correlation declines to 0.4 in college students.[3] The decline in correlation proves more factors are in play. Your academic success isn't predetermined. Even though I'm not a doctor, you can see genetics are not the only factor that plays into academic success.

My parents weren't the best in academics as young adults. They were average students, averaging Bs sometimes Cs throughout high school. If I went straight off genetics then I would just be that, an average student. Growing up, I didn't show too much natural intelligence, either.

For instance, I mumbled a lot. The mumbling got so bad that my parents got me a speech therapist. The speech therapist's goal was to teach me how to talk clearer. I need to articulate more so people could understand me.

During classes, I would consistently drift off. I would go up into my headspace, thinking about who knows what. I was a thinker, daydreamer if you will. When I did this, I would have this blank stare upon my face. The best way to describe this face is if you imagine someone saying "duhhh" out loud. Also, picture them while staring off into the distance with a blank stare. That was me, being made fun of continuously for looking stupid and acting foolishly.

I was terrible at grammar and below average in reading. I was a slow reader. Pronouncing longer, harder words was also a pitfall of mine, damaging my confidence. And my academic performance showed. I struggled in early academics. The struggle and doubt got bad enough that I ended up getting tutors to try to increase my abilities in school.

My confidence started to rise by my late middle school years. For some magical reason, I began to get good grades in math. I don't know what happened. I just started to get it, and I liked it. I carried that success and momentum with me into high school. By my freshman year, I was lucky enough to find a group of top-achieving friends. Their intelligence blew me out of the water. I was the only one not enrolled in advanced level courses. However, they pushed me to join these advanced math classes so that we could be in the same room together.

To my shock and everyone else's surprise, I excelled in these classes. My attitude changed. I started building upon my triumphs, acquiring momentum and confidence along the way. This experience put me on a pathway to a very prosperous college career. I was able to change my path from an average student to a straight-A, Summa Cum Laude college graduate.

I didn't accept the fact that my parents were only average students or the possibility that I had bad genetics. I didn't let my early struggles with reading and spelling define my future. I changed my mindset and environment and put in the work. The success followed.

I worked hard in college. I had a strict focus on maintaining a high GPA. However, many people would tell me, "Wow, you're so lucky, I wish I had your genes" or "You're lucky you're gifted." Every time I heard someone belittle my hard work, I tried to not let it get to me. They just didn't know. Don't be one of those people who believe that success is a lucky gift. More importantly, don't be one who listens to them.

Every student can learn; your level of "natural intelligence" doesn't matter. Intelligence is an adaptive function of your brain. You have the power to be a better student, the best student! Don't be trapped by the perception of genetics and fate; you control your destiny and your success.

Myth #2: I don't have time to be successful

It was only a couple of days away until my college career began, and I would start my first college-level class. I began to get a little nervous and didn't know what to expect. I was living by myself in an on-campus apartment, and some anxiety started to kick in. I decided to go for a walk to calm myself down. As I took a stroll around campus, I tried to understand where all my classes were. Around 30 minutes into my journey, I ran into an upperclassman sitting on an outside bench.

We got to talking. I told him a little about myself: where I was from, what high school I went to, where I live on campus, and my expected major. We chatted for a while, and before he walked off, I asked him if he had any advice for me as an incoming freshman. He stopped, thought for a couple of seconds, and chuckled. He said, "Learn to balance the college triangle."

the college triangle
PARADOX

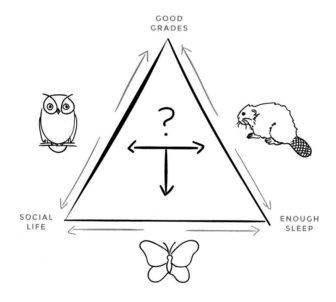

A visual representation of a triangle explains the paradox. The three leading time spenders for college students are in each corner of a triangle. The three corners are sufficient sleep, good grades, and social life. The graphic shows that as you move closer to a specific side, you lose availability to the other. Each side, a student picks, establishes a persona that has some advantages.

Furthermore, these personas also have glaring disadvantages. I went against the grain and decided that this paradox wasn't valid. I didn't believe that this was the only way. However, if you believe in the "College Triangle," these are the three personas available to you:

The Busy Beaver: Beavers are one of the most active, hardworking animals in the animal kingdom. Busy Beavers spend most of their time with academics, studying all the time, while still focusing on getting a full night's sleep. Social life will be virtually nonexistent because they spend their time alone. Busy Beavers are also regarded as being anti-social.

The Social Butterfly: Butterflies tend to find safety in numbers and are usually seen in groups. Social Butterflies spend most of the time building relationships and meeting new people. They also tend to involve themselves in various student organizations and activities. They're attending social events and parties, still maintaining enough sleep whenever they can get it to stay well-rested. Academics are in the back of the Social Butterfly's mind and results usually turn disastrous.

The Night Owl: Owls are nocturnal animals and are usually up during the late hours of the day and early morning. Night Owls spend most of their time with friends and various student organizations. They're friendly and fun to be around. They still know the importance of school and obtaining good grades. They'll tend to force themselves to work late at night for studying and writing papers. They're okay with pulling all-nighters. They start to lose out on sleep more often than not, and it starts to stack up.

All three personas have glaring negatives that will have serious implications. A lot of people perceive the Busy Beaver as the goal or the model student. I would believe that most parents preach this type of behavior to their kids before going to college, to focus on grades and not partying. Although academics should be the primary focus, social intelligence is as relevant.

In the real world, employers will look for both academic and social capabilities—academics and sociability play critical roles in securing a job after college. The high GPA helps your resume stand out and will assist in getting that vital interview. When a college student lands an interview, most of the time, the meeting is for the employer to see if they'll fit: Do you fit their culture and values? Can you hold conversations? Can you work well in a group? How do you deal with disputes with other people? They want to find out if their team can work with you and vice versa. Employers have a common question in the back of their minds, "Can you spend a whole day in a car/airport together?" Social skills are essential.

Having a social life in college is a great stress reliever. Getting your mind off the daily grind and the wear and tear classwork is crucial. Clearing your mind and having fun outside of school is critical. That's why colleges have various opportunities to meet new people. They all mitigate stress. Most of my fondest memories of college were due to the social life I had. It makes college fun. It helps build relationships and memories that will last through generations. Most academic-minded people see the social side of college as a distraction. However, meeting new people will have a lifetime worth of benefits.

Social interactions have plenty of health benefits, as well. Psychologists have found that direct contact will trigger parts of our nervous system to release numerous neurotransmitters. These neurotransmitters will regulate our stress and anxiety levels. Also, social interaction releases dopamine. Dopamine is known to make people feel joyful and reduce pain. Just by talking and interacting with people, you can reduce stress, anxiety, and feel good.

Research links social motivation and social contact to improved memory and recall functions of the brain. It also protects your brain from neurodegenerative diseases like Parkinson's disease. Also, seniors who live a social life that prioritizes social goals have higher late-life satisfaction.[4] Social interaction makes us happier and healthier in the present and the future. Be social and prioritize it.

Being social also has a professional benefit that can boost your career. Have you ever heard of the expression "It isn't what you know, it's who you know"?

This saying applies a lot in life. References, referrals, recommendations, are opened up to you with the relationships you form. Opportunities you never thought were possible will come to fruition. Don't take this lightly; open up and meet new people. The benefits will come.

Social Butterflies are the most popular choice.

As I mentioned, these students put academics on the backburner. It's the most popular because it takes the least amount of work. It's a relaxed attitude, and missing classes is common. They tend to sit in the back of the classroom (sometimes sleeping). They miss assignments and struggle taking tests. Sure, they'll have a blast in college. They'll have friends, memories, and experiences, but their grades are usually abysmal. They may even struggle to graduate.

With a mediocre to low GPA and no academic references, these social butterflies will struggle during their job search. Finding a good-paying job in the area they want will be difficult. Grades show employers that you know how to work. Hardworking is a critical trait that employers look for in potential employees. They want to see if you're capable of getting the work they give you done well. When they examine your resume with a low GPA, they'll most likely disregard it or throw it in the trash. Even though most employers look for sociability, academic success proves your work ethic. If you cannot portray a positive work ethic to potential employers, you'll have no chance to show off your social skills. Poor grades make finding a well-paying job after college an uphill battle. Level the field, put in the work now, and focus on grades.

Finally, the night owl is the persona that's the most dangerous to your health. In the short term, this position will work and may work well, but problems will occur. In maintaining this persona over a long period, your health will suffer. Quality sleep is essential to your health.

When you sleep, your brain goes through this cleaning procedure. The more "cleaning" your brain gets, the more your learning and memory processes will improve. Sleep energizes the body and the mind. Visualize that your brain calls in a cleaning crew to come in when you go to sleep. This crew's job is to do a thorough cleaning of your mind, wiping all the walls and floors down, and putting all the junk away and organized. Everything is spotless and shiny for the next day. Doing all the work needed. Therefore, you have to give this hypothetical cleaning crew enough time to do this work.

According to the National Institute of Neurological Disorders and Stroke, the average adult needs 7 to 9 hours of sound sleep every night. Getting that 7 to 9 hours helps with the following:

- Reducing stress levels
- Improving your immune system
- Maintaining a healthy body weight
- Lowering the risk of future health problems
- Reducing irritability
- Ability to think clearer (Reduce brain fog)[5]

Without sleep, you can't form or maintain the critical pathways in your brain that let you learn and create new memories. It's harder to concentrate and quickly respond with a mind that's lacking good sleep. Night owls might find success in the short term, but successive sleepless nights will add up. Lack of sleep will hinder your academic and social progress. Grades will start to slip, and irritability will begin to rise.

The night owl persona is the most dangerous because of the potential for mental and physical health problems. Sometimes, circumstances dictate your schedule. Work begins to pile up, and there's no option except to push through the late hours of the night. I found it's best to find a spot to cut off from all schoolwork, go to bed, and wake up early to finish. I tend to get better results working after a good night's sleep. The results from cramming sessions while tired or overstimulated on caffeine are poor. Make sleep a priority and stick to it.

In addition to academics, social lives, and sleep, there's also a fourth dimension to this dilemma. This fourth part, often ignored, is essential to mention: student-athletes and students with jobs. Both of these types of students have a fourth category that they need to balance. Whether it's athletics or a job, they both take up multiple hours a week. Juggling all four of these aspects may seem impossible, but here's the thing: it still can be done.

I played on our university's baseball team. Playing baseball consisted of a fall and spring season. The fall was our out-of-season schedule, and the spring was our in-season schedule. In the fall, we woke up each morning at 6 am to work out for an hour and a half. In the afternoons, we had practice lasting around three hours. In the spring, we had one to two games during the weekdays and three games every weekend. If a game started at 5 pm, we had to get there before 2 pm, and then we hopefully leave the field by 9 pm. Also, we needed travel time for away games. A vast amount of time was spent on a bus and in hotel rooms during our in-season schedule.

Even though baseball took up a ton of my time, it wasn't everything for me. I was also very active outside of my baseball schedule and team activities. I joined a couple of organizations in the business college. In these organizations, I made some new friends not associated with athletics. I was able to meet my wife, Ashley, through these social activities. I would have never met this wonderful person if I focused on only academics or athletics. I met so many people throughout my four years.

I also focused on getting at least 8 hours of sleep. I needed many hours to operate efficiently throughout my days. I wasn't able to sustain a consistent 8 hours of sleep every night. Therefore, I would plan on which days I could sleep in and schedule bedtime like an appointment.

Finally, on top of that, I ended up graduating with a double major in accounting and finance in four years with a 4.0 GPA. This result isn't to "toot my own horn" but to illustrate that balancing this lifestyle is possible and can be done.

Blocking Your Time

At first, it's hard to remember all the things you have to do and when to do them. The strategy that many productive people use is time blocking. Time blocking is when you divide your day into predetermined allotments of time. I started by creating a master list of tasks. What needs to be on this list? Well, do you have a to-do list? Have homework that needs doing? Upcoming tests that will you need to study for? A party coming up? A new movie you want to see? Anything and everything that requires time needs to be on this master list at a minimum. Get as fancy and organized as you like.

Next to each item on the list, place the date that you need to complete the task. Estimate the amount of time necessary to complete. If a task is too big, break it up into smaller segments.

Each smaller segment will be done on different days with smaller amounts of time to complete. Subdivide as many times as you want.

Before you go to bed, go through your list and throw in tasks in your schedule for tomorrow. Set a start and end time for each task with the amount of time you estimated for completion. Block out your day, every minute. If there's still free time in the day, always figure out what you want to do during those gaps. Knowing you have free time will allow you to be more productive during the times you blocked off. This discipline gives you focus and a purpose to complete tasks because of the upcoming reward of open time.

Time blocking will organize the tasks that need to be completed and allow 100% focus on each task. A chart is shown demonstrating how your estimation accuracy will improve with experience. At first, your estimates have a high likelihood of being off; however, they'll improve with experience. Make constant adjustments to your estimating procedure. Be kind to yourself; you'll get better at estimating the more you do it. You'll soon find out you'll become more realistic the more you do it.

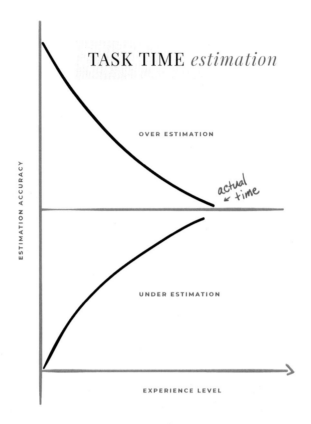

TASK TIME *estimation*

OVER ESTIMATION

actual
← *time*

ESTIMATION ACCURACY

UNDER ESTIMATION

EXPERIENCE LEVEL

Perfection isn't the goal here. There's a buffer to this estimating process called Parkinson's Law. Parkinson's Law is that "work expands to fill the time available for its completion." The time to complete a task will adjust in order to fill the time frame given. Time blocking forces you to commit to your priorities; also, it helps you balance your urgent and essential tasks.[6] Time blocking also tackles one of college students' biggest problems: procrastination.

Take advantage of time blocking. It will make balancing academics, social life, sleep, and work/athletics possible. Numerous books and articles have been written on how to time block. If you need a bigger explanation or more strategies, please take the time to research them. A book that really helped me with time management and prioritization is *The One Thing* by Gary Keller. I suggest taking the time to read the wisdom that book brings.

No more being busy beavers, social butterflies, or night owls. Possibilities are endless; all it takes is mastering your time.

Chapter 1 Summary

- Eliminate the two common myths hindering your success in college:
  - o There are more important factors that go into good grades than genetics.
  - o You have the ability to do more with your day; control your time.
- Genetics is just a small contributor to your success.
  - o Focus on your mental health, environment, and work ethic.
- Don't let past and current struggles define your future.
- The College Triangle: Academics, Social Life, and Sleep
  - o All three serve important functions to the overall college experience.
  - o Academics: Good grades prove strong work ethic.
  - o Social Life: Demonstrates strong people skills and charisma.
  - o Sleep: Promotes a healthy mind and body.
  - o Student Athletes/Employed Students add a 4th dimension.
  - o It's possible to have it all, only with focused planned determination.
- Time blocking is a great strategy to maximize time productivity and focus.
- Constantly improve on your task time estimations.
- Divide your days with tasks and work that needs to be done.
- Plan for relaxation and social opportunities.

THE WINNER'S MINDSET

You have complete control over your success. Genetics and luck have nothing to do with your possible success. Since you have a new appreciation for your time, it's time to work on the winner's mindset. Remove any other limiting beliefs you have in your life. Negative thoughts and words have no benefit to you; transition to a positive mindset. It will build the foundation and establish the groundwork for victory.

Put your right foot forward in the direction of progress. Setting your mind up for success is a high starting point for positive change; do it. You have to honestly believe that you can be and have the time to be successful.

Positivity is Key

I would like you to do a little exercise. First, check and see if you're alone. If you're not alone, find a room with privacy, and go there. A bathroom is perfect. Once you're at that location, stand up, walk over to a mirror, stare yourself in the face and boldly say: "I am smart, and I have time to be successful." Say it again, louder. "I am smart, and I have time to be successful!" Now say it a third time, even louder and bolder. "I AM SMART, AND I HAVE TIME TO BE SUCCESSFUL!" Let it sink in, embrace this saying. Let it be a part of your essence. A portion of your makeup. A part of YOU!

A lot of naysayers find positive self-talk to be frilly and a bunch of "mumbo jumbo." When it was first suggested to me to do more positive self-talk, I remember rolling my eyes back. Like talking to myself would make a difference at all. How can telling myself, "I can do it," change anything about the situation? With all this doubt, I put my pride and ego aside and humored the idea of positive self-talk. Lo and behold, it changed my perception and my ability more than I could ever imagine. Positive self-talk opened a world of possibilities for me.

It makes the impossible seem possible. It makes the most daunting tasks achievable. If I were to go back in time and tell my teenage self that I would write a book in my mid-twenties, I would have laughed in my face. All it took me to write this book was an idea that I wanted to share, and someone saying, "You should write a book." Rather than just brushing that comment off and thinking, "I'm no writer; I'm a math kid. I struggle to write a 5-page essay, let alone a whole book." I said to myself, "I can do it!" So I did.

Positive self-talk opens the mind up to many possibilities. Negative self-talk closes the door. The way you use positive self-talk can be unique to you based on what works best. Try different methods such as referring yourself in the second or even third person (you vs. your name or he/she), having self-talk in either the instructional or motivating frame. The only guideline for this is that it has to be in a positive light.

Even though research is relatively new, the experts at the Mayo Clinic say that positive self-talk may lead to:

- Increased life span
- Lower rates of depression

- Lower levels of distress
- Better mental and physical well-being
- Better cardiovascular health and reduced risk of death from cardio-vascular disease
- Better coping skills during hardships and times of stress.[7]

Helpful Hint: Before tests, to boost my confidence, I would stand in a power pose for two minutes. A power pose is anything a superhero like Superman or Wonder Woman would do: Chest out, chin up, eyes determined, and hands on hips. The Power Pose is a "life hack" proposed by Amy Cuddy. For more information, watch her TED talk: Your body language may shape who you are.

Visualize Your Championship

It's time to take the positive self-talk a step further and visualize success. What will it look like when you succeed? How will you feel? Try to imagine it. Play it in your head like a movie of your success. Now make that picture bigger, brighter, louder. Visualizing success is yet another everyday activity among successful people.

Athletes, actors/actresses, entrepreneurs, and everyone in between all do it. A brain is a powerful tool. If you can already decide and know how you'll succeed, it's more likely that you'll be successful than not.

When I was in college, I decided early on that I was going to get good grades and graduate with honors. I used to picture myself during graduation with thousands of people all around me. I was walking down the aisle. Wearing my black cap and gown, with gold cords draped around my neck and hearing my name walking across the stage and receiving my diploma that said summa cum laude on it. Whenever I was battling difficult times in school, I would just play that tape over and over in my head.

That visualization came true. The power of positive self-talk and visualizing success is very valuable. This should be practiced regularly. It's the essence of the groundwork. The rest of the book will be meaningless if you genuinely don't believe you can succeed in college and see yourself doing it.

The final helpful mindset trick is to answer a couple of questions before doing any schoolwork, such as attending class, homework, studying, projects, anything involving the school. Every student should know and eternalize their "why" and "how." More specifically, they need to know the answers to these questions: "Why am I learning this?" and "How can I teach this to someone else?" The answers to these questions have to be genuine and thorough.

The "Why"

"Why am I learning this?" is an essential question on many levels. Finding and defining your personal "why" is the most critical thing you can do when starting to learn something new. It's the purpose, the drive to push you to do the work. This answer will motivate you when things get tough. Even though it doesn't seem like it, there are two levels to this question. The "why" is broken up into two parts:

Why are you attending college in the first place? And why are you taking this specific class or learning this particular topic?

Ingrain the "why" for college in your mind. You're spending tens of thousands of dollars to obtain a piece of paper primarily. Understand why you're starting college and why you'll graduate will give you purpose. This thinking will create your intention that will drive you to that finish line. Throughout my life, I've heard many wrong reasons for why someone is going to or attending college.

For example, the following are some of the most popular reasons I have heard. My parents wanted me to attend college. I didn't know what else to do next in my life, so I'm going to college. It looks like a fun time and is what everyone does. These reasons are shallow and won't fuel your drive. When things start getting tough and challenging, these people will mentally check out. A strong "why" needs to be discovered and understood. If not, most students will struggle and either drop out or fail out.

On the one hand, attaining a good job and making a good salary is a decent reason to begin with when starting college. On the other hand, as you get further into college, that reason has to be more specific and personal for it to be effective in securing an excellent job in that particular field, doing precisely what, for what exact reasons. The more specific and personal, the more impact it will have on you. When I was in college, I had a dual purpose of graduating. I wanted to prove to myself and others that I was smarter than they thought. I wanted to have the skills necessary to be a sought-after employee after I graduated, while knowing that someday, I would take these skills back to my family company and add value. After you develop a "why" for attending college, it's time to break down the "why" to the class level.

Now I understand that for some classes, it might be hard to find the "why." It might be an elective or a mandatory course that you know you're going to hate and never use in your life. Whatever the backstory is doesn't matter; what matters is finding that "why."

During my junior year, I signed up for an online class called "Introduction to Geology." This class was to meet my elective science criteria needed for graduation. I couldn't care less about rocks and minerals, and being online gave me more of an excuse not to care.

After the first couple of weeks, I started to struggle in that class. At one point, this geology class was my lowest grade in all of my classes! I went to my dad and explained that I just hated this class and had no desire to learn anything regarding it. It's stupid that I even have to take this class as a business major.

He told me that geology was part of my family history. My great grandfather was fascinated by rocks and gemstones. He collected them throughout the years of his life. My father then said that taking this class would help me understand more about my family history. That may seem like a stretch to correlate an online geology class to understand my family history. Nonetheless, it was all the meaning I needed. I ended up passing and getting an A in that class.

If you're having difficulty finding the answer to this question, humor yourself. The only rule is that it has to be somewhat genuine. Another option or a fallback is to reference the matter differently. Why is this professor teaching this? Why do they do this for a living? Answering someone else's "why" through your perspective might generate enough meaning to translate to you; you can then use it for your motivation and purpose.

The "How"

Now that you have the "why," next is the "how." The "how" is usually overlooked when it comes to student preparation. You need to ask yourself this question multiple times throughout every class. "How can I teach this to someone else?" This question is a powerful one that isn't too well known yet.

I had to do a lot of tutoring throughout college. I was approached and asked by classmates to help them study for or complete assignments. I put a personal emphasis on being kind, friendly, and smart (or at least perceived smart). Because of this, I had a habit of saying yes to these requests. I created stress and pressure because I didn't want to let these people down. During class and while doing my work, I always had to think, "How can I teach this?" I knew I had classmates interested in me helping them study. I felt somewhat responsible for their success.

Asking yourself this question transitions you from "learning apprentice" to "expert." To teach something, you have to not only memorize something but also know and understand it. By asking this question, you're already deciding that you'll learn the material soon. In a way, it tricks your brain.

Also, reviewing this question will cause you to analyze the material and organize it in your brain more efficiently. This way, you can preface the information in a way you can easily explain. You'll make your summaries and explanations. This technique will cement the material in your brain, not only helping yourself but others as well. So, know your "why" and understand your "how."

The Never-Ending Mindset

The expression "mind-over-matter," is a common phrase used in athletics. It's used to show that willpower can overcome physical problems and challenges in your life. The mind is a powerful thing. If you understand how to use it to your advantage, it can propel you past any obstacle life throws at you. Having the right mindset and excellent will power isn't a "one and done" deal. You have to keep improving and growing it time and time again. Life will throw you curveballs, and if you aren't ready, it will set you back.

A constant growth mindset is always needed. Don't develop destination disease. You'll never "arrive" in life. Once complacency develops, regression and failure will surely follow. If you're green, you're growing. If you're ripe, you'll rot. Establish, maintain, and always improve that winner's mindset. This mindset of positivity and purpose will set you up for success. Keep up with them and make these a part of your daily life. Success will follow.

Chapter 2 Summary

- Having a positive mindset should be your first priority.
  - o Keep finding ways to grow and stay positive.
  - o Start and end each day, reflecting upon what's currently right in your life or what you're thankful for.
- You're smart and have the ability to be successful.
- Positivity has many benefits to your health, well-being, and performance:
  - o There are many types of positive self-talk.
  - o Try out different methods and see what works for you.
- Visualizing your future success like it's a movie, already created: play that movie over and over again in your mind.
  - o Make it vivid; make it real.
- Answer these two questions before you do any schoolwork:
  - o Why am I learning this?
  - o How can I teach this to someone else?
- Know your why and make it as truthful and believable as possible.
- The teaching mindset makes your brain work differently to make information accessible to you in a way that's easier to recall and explain.
- Mind over matter, always look for that next challenge. Stack your successes.
  - o Growth mindset: There's always room for improvement.

CHAPTER 3

THE MASTER'S ENVIRONMENT

N ow that you have your mind set up for success, it's time to build a quality environment around you. Your environment is all the aspects in your life that you have influence over and can change.

One aspect is the people you surround yourself with regularly such as your friends and family. Building your class-A environment is important. The people you're around most can impact how you think, feel, and act. This phenomenon is called herd mentality. Herd mentality is the tendency for people's actions and behaviors to be altered or influenced by their peers. This is something completely different than peer pressure. The more time you spend with the same group of people, the more your thoughts, words, and actions will align. That's why it's important to be intentional with whom you spend your time. Your future depends on it.

We Are Tribal

We are tribal creatures in nature. We crave to be a part of a group and accepted by that group. It's in our DNA. Throughout the history of the human race, mankind has evolved through the aid of small groups. These small groups are also known as tribes. Even though countries are becoming more individualistic, people have tribal roots. These roots cannot be ignored.

People's social identity and their desire for belonging run deep within their psyches. From the beginning, human species started forming groups for their protection and security. They came together for growth. The whole premise behind languages is to facilitate interacting within groups. People needed a more advanced way of communicating; thus, they invented language.

Thus, we come to the idea of the "social identity theory." This theory is widely accepted in the psychology world. This theory demonstrates that people's sense of who they are is based on their group membership. The social identity theory has three stages: categorization, identification, and comparison.

Categorization, simply put, is when we try to see groups in society and attach our own category to them. Categorization is used in order to understand the current social environment in nature. We do this in an attempt to match groups with categories within ourselves. This leads into the second phase called identification. This is when we adopt the identity of the group we've categorized ourselves as belonging to. We identify this as one of our in-groups. This step has an emotional component. Identification affects our sense of belongingness and self-esteem most.

Finally, the last stage is comparison when we compare the group we're in with other groups. We start to compare our in-groups with the other groups called out-groups. This comparison is used as a validation and development of our own hierarchy system in our own minds.[8] I don't want to go too deep into social identity and the dynamics of in-groups and out-groups.

However, it's important to know it on a surface level in order to understand our natural behaviors.

Social identity theory is displayed all around us. We see examples of it every day. This is one reason why sports teams are so popular with fan bases and why rivalries are so important. This is why prejudices and racism are formed in society. Also, this is why the Mafia and gang violence are huge parts of U.S. history and still in effect today. Social identity and tribalism are big parts of our past, present, and future.

The sense of belonging is a strong motivator in people. People feel connected, supported, and respected when someone feels that they belong. Trust levels rise and confidence in day-to-day activities grow. Students who feel like they belong and are valued by a group of peers are able to engage more in learning.[9]

This is yet another reason why establishing a strong group or tribe is important. Surround yourself with people who will have a positive influence on you. Surround yourself with people who have drive, a solid work ethic, and self-respect. They don't have to be geniuses, just people who want to do something bigger than themselves. Ultimately, whomever you surround yourself with should care for your success. You should care for their success as well.

Attracting the Right People

Now how do I know if the people I meet will be good for my success? A good rule of thumb is would your grandparents approve of them? This may seem silly, but older generations have great judgement of character because they've been around and interacted with people longer. They can see right through the nonsense and get right to the core of people. I was always nervous whenever bringing friends around my grandparents because they always told me how it was. They never sugar coated anything.

A good strategy is to connect with people who have a similar major or classes as you have. This way, you can study and work on assignments together. You'll also have someone who can relate to you and the challenges you're experiencing. You have a built-in support group when you build your environment like this. Having people you can talk to, who can empathize with your challenges, will make you feel like you're not alone, making you stronger.

I attended a very small elementary school. When I say small, I mean tiny. It was a preschool to 8th grade school and each grade averaged 10 to 15 kids. Even though all the kids were from many different towns, everyone knew everyone. We were around each other so much that we all naturally got along. A strong bond existed between the students at that school. This school also had the reputation of expanding students' abilities to new heights. They attributed this to the high teacher-to-student ratio. Even though the learning environment was intense, all the students were getting an excellent education.

After my 4th grade year, my parents transferred me to our hometown public school. At first, I didn't make too many friends in middle school. I'm naturally an introvert and kept to myself often. Despite that, I still tried to talk and play games with other kids. I made some friends through my middle school years, but not until high school did I meet my true friends.

During middle school, my average grade was a B. Not bad but not great. The group of friends I made during band camp helped me become successful in high school and college. My group of friends consisted of honor students and National Honor Society members. This group also included our class's president, vice president, and five valedictorians. I was none of these.

These people subconsciously pushed my abilities. They morphed my behavior into a person that had increased drive and success in school. I graduated in the top 10% of my class and was able to get a five on the AP Calculus test. The bonus was my friends never made me feel inferior and didn't push me to be smarter. Just being constantly around them made me better.

Unfortunately, none of my close friends from high school attended the same college as me. I had to develop a new group of friends. After only a couple weeks, I was lucky enough to meet a handful of great people. Most of them were business majors. They all had a desire to graduate college with an impressive resume, like myself. This included achieving a high GPA, completing internships, and involvement in college organizations.

I started to spend a lot of my time with this group of friends. We would study for tests and try to schedule future classes together. Our relationships weren't only focused around school. Every so often, we would hang out and have a good time; nevertheless, our main focus was to get through school.

Study/homework sessions turned into teaching/tutoring sessions. There was no judgment in our group because everyone at one point needed help or a push in the right direction. I credit a lot of my success in school to other people. I know for a fact that I wouldn't have achieved the same level of success in college if it hadn't been for these friends.

You can travel farther in life with the aid of other people. Find people who have a desire for success and surround yourself with them. Eliminate toxic people who will only drag you down to their level. Add driven, positive people. The tribe you establish and surround yourself with is important to you. Your success depends on it.

This isn't some New Age idea. One of the oldest books ever written is the Bible and it talks about the influence others have on someone. Proverbs 12:26 states, "The righteous choose their friends carefully, but the way of the wicked leads them astray." This Bible verse tells us that morally right people will be careful about whom they surround themselves with. They know the influence people have on one another. Righteous people know that the wrong people will lead them off the path of greatness.

Find Your Sacred Spaces

In addition to the people in your life, the second part of your environment includes your sacred spaces, which are your "go-to" locations you use to be alone for personal improvement. Sacred spaces are spots special to you that you can easily get to and do the work needed. This includes studying, practicing, reflecting, meditating, or any other self-improvement activity.

When I was in college, I had two sacred spaces. The first one was a particular table at the school's library on a quiet floor by a window that overlooked a very beautiful part of campus. The library was never packed, especially on the quiet floors. I was able to go to this space and do work. I would study here, do homework here, write papers here, and anything else I needed to do for school.

My second sacred spot was my desk in my bedroom. I used this when I had to practice something vocal, like a speech. It was also my fallback when my table at the library was taken or closed. Besides these two sacred spots, I also used study pods in the business college for group studying or when the work I was doing wasn't urgent.

The sacred spaces are used for personal quiet time, where no one can bother you. You can do the work that needs to be done. So, find a couple spots where you can easily and repeatedly get to and that mean something to you. Also, the reason why these spots are sacred is that they shouldn't have distractions. Stay away from social media platforms, TVs, and your phones (for personal/social uses that don't facilitate studying) as much as possible. Use these spots and don't let other people or distractions pollute your sacred spaces. If you need to group study or work with someone else, find a different spot. These sacred spaces are yours and shouldn't be shared. Develop these spots and use them frequently.

Chapter 3 Summary

- The people we surround ourselves with influence us through their actions and thoughts.
- Be careful and intentional about whom you surround yourself with.
- Surround yourself with people who will have a positive influence on you.
- Find your sacred spaces and keep them holy.
- Sacred spaces are yours and are where you'll get the most work done.

THE CHAMPION'S WORK ETHIC

After establishing a positive mindset and a successful environment, it's time to do the work. This is the last piece of the groundwork puzzle. Personal drive and hard work are necessities for a successful college life. For example, graduating college with honors takes diligent, regimented, hard work. This uses a lot of energy. With all the classes, assignments, and tests, the effort needed to perform at a high level is second to none.

Work ethic is required in other areas of life besides college; nothing in life worth achieving comes with ease. Think about a couple of your proudest accomplishments in your life. The goals you achieved. Now reflect on all the work, struggles, and failures that happened to you along the way.

Every baseball award I received was a result of the work I put in: years of agonizing work out sessions, countless practices, and lessons as well as the many failures along the way. In college, I spent hours studying, writing, doing assignments, tutoring, practicing problems, etc. Hard work is necessary for any accomplishment.

I was lucky enough to be in several interviews and eventually be a part of a company's hiring process. Hardworking is a top trait companies look for when hiring new personnel. GPA shows not only how smart you are but also how hard you work. Keep this in mind when going through college. Developing a strong worth ethic will stick with you throughout your life. It will also give you opportunities for future achievements. There's always light at the end of the tunnel. Keep working hard and push yourself.

There are two sides to everything. You have to be careful not to burn out by working too hard for too long. Your drive fizzles away. Your once strong work ethic leaves. College burnout can be disastrous and can derail a successful college career. I saw the writing on the wall early on in college when I saw seniors, whom I looked up to, give up and stopped trying. I had to avoid burnout at all costs. On one hand, I knew there was nothing I could do to make college *easy*. On the other hand, there had to be a way to make it *less difficult*.

Work Smarter, Not Harder

There's a common phrase used in manufacturing: Work smarter, not harder. To demonstrate this saying, I'll give a real-life example. A woman working for a manufacturer is responsible for making a specific widget. The job entails taking a sheet of metal, placing it into the press, and cycling the press. It takes around 10 seconds for the press to cycle. She then needs to take the part out, do a quick quality check, place the part in the box, and repeat. In order to make her quota, she has to produce 1,000 pieces in an 8-hour shift. That translates to around 140 pieces an hour, if you take into consideration break times and defective pieces.

There isn't too much room for error if she produces the part exactly how I described it. She'll have to work very hard for the whole 8-hour shift to make quota. By the end of the shift, she'll be exhausted. It will be hard for her to maintain that work ethic every day. However, if she comes up with a better process to make the part, then she won't have to work as strenuously.

Let's say she checks the widget and stages the sheets of metal during the press cycle time. Saving 10 whole seconds. When the press is done, she immediately takes out the part and inserts the next piece of steel. She starts the press again, with hardly any press idle time. That means she can get a part every 12 or so seconds which averages to 300 pieces an hour. By just changing the process, she was able to get around double the output, with no extra work.

That example demonstrates the goal of this book. There's always a better way to do something. Even though it may take some experimenting and trial and error, you can always find a better way. Thinking outside the box and figuring out what works best for you is key. This innovative way of thinking is how humanity was able to progress throughout history. Most inventions were created because somebody knew there was a better way, so they figured it out.

In the early 15th century there was no good way to mass produce books for the population. At the time, monks had to painstakingly copy pages by hand. As you can imagine, this was extremely labor intensive and took a lot of time. Books were then hard to come by and extremely expensive. Few could even afford to acquire books. Johannes Gutenberg knew there had to be a better way to copy and print books. Gutenberg didn't accept this reality and eventually came up with a better way to mass produce books. This made books cheaper and allowed more people to have access to books. Thus, the printing press was invented. The printing press sparked a revolution in Europe in the mid-15th century.

At the beginning of the 20th century, Henry Ford saw that the then current way to build and assemble cars took an inordinate amount of time. The labor costs alone made cars so expensive that the average citizen couldn't afford one. Ford saw this and thought there had to be a better way. In 1913, the assembly line was created, which vastly improved production time and cut cost drastically. This too sparked a revolution that changed how industry, countrywide, operated.

While these examples are on a large scale and sparked revolutions, they both have a common theme. Both Gutenberg and Ford didn't accept the status quo. They both knew there was a better way of doing something, so they figured it out. This book will show a method to improve the process of studying. These study methods will help you work smarter and not harder to get success.

Now this may not spark a world revolution, but it may spark an internal one. Even though the methods in this book may make it easier to succeed, you still need to put in the work. Just as people still need to work hard printing books and manufacturing cars, you'll still need to work hard to obtain good grades.

Success is Scheduled

Time is important. It's one of the most valuable assets to a college student. A college student can have a lot of work and activities on their plate. They all take up a lot of time in a week. A five-day week has 120 hours. Of that 120 hours, take out 40 hours of sleeping (8 hours a day is what you should be getting), and 15 hours for your classes (a typical course load per semester). That leaves you with 65 hours a week to do whatever you want, 13 hours a day. College is about making the best use of those 13 hours. They should be as productive as possible.

As mentioned before, block out those 13 hours, either each morning or before bedtime. If you need to do an assignment, figure out when. If you want to eat lunch with friends, put it on the schedule. If you need to study for a test, block off the time. The weekends should be used as an overflow. I tried to do as little schoolwork as possible on the weekends. Weekends, for me, were used for rest, relaxation, and bonding time with friends.

Most procrastination happens when people put things off till the weekend. Weekends might seem like a good time to do your work because they have a lot of open time. However, something always happens that could take priority over work. Use weekends for rest and relaxation. Try to plan to get all your work done during the weekdays. Success is scheduled, so plan accordingly.

Early on, studying for tests was the biggest time commitment for me in college. It took the most time, and it was hard to plan how much time was needed to study. That's when I thought there had to be a better, smarter way to study. The following section will demonstrate the method I used in college. These methods will help improve studying, increase retention, and, most importantly, save time. When I came up with this method, I was able to break up studying into a couple sessions.

Once I mastered this method, I only needed a couple of hours outside of the classroom to prepare for tests. This efficiency may not come right away. Sticking to it, however, will reduce studying time to this small amount. You will no longer need to spend countless hours reading textbooks. No more scouring through unorganized notes to try to cram for a test. The next section will cover the legwork, which will be broken down in phases. Read through, follow, and stick to these phases; then watch how you'll save time and study smarter.

Chapter 4 Summary

- Success takes hard work; there's no way around it.
- No one ever said college will be easy, but it can be less difficult.
- Work smarter, not harder.
    o Have a mindset that there's always a better way to do something.
- Time is very valuable, plan for your success.
- Improvements will come if you stick with your process.
    o Repetition is the key for improvement.

SECTION 2

THE LEGWORK

There are two sides to every coin. Success comes from the balance and mastery of both sides. Chinese culture expresses this through a complex relational concept called Yin and Yang. This is a perfect example to show the balance of two opposing yet complementing ideas. In this book, these are the groundwork and the legwork. The mindset and philosophies versus the actions and practices. Both are different in many ways but also complementary to each other. Success is dependent on both.

At this time, you should have a basic understanding of the groundwork. This showed how to establish your personal foundation for your college career. You have also eliminated the two common myths deterring success in college. You have a new, bright, and positive mindset and a picture of your future success. You've established a supportive group of friends and colleagues. Sacred spaces were developed to conduct your work. You now have an appreciation of your time and the notion that there's always a better way of doing something. With all those installed in your life, the groundwork is set, understood, and in place. It's time to discuss the legwork.

I'll now present you with five steps or phases to efficiently and effectively study in college. You have the choice of either starting with the first topic, master it. Or you can read through these five steps, find the area that fascinates you the most, and start with that. It can be used as a process or a series of choices; it's up to you.

I know you've tried systems of studying in the past that didn't work. We all have. An approach you should take to this book is to find out why those didn't work and decide to do something different. Integrate those realizations into these practices. You have the wisdom regarding processes. Set yourself up for success. Any procedure will work if you adopt it; no procedure will work if you don't adopt it.

I've fine-tuned these steps throughout my years in college. The personal experiences I had, good or bad, made me analyze this process. The more I did this process the better I became at studying. I was faster, used a lot less energy, and got more success from it. Each step has its own goals that adds to a student's studying experience. Everyone's brain is wired differently, and everyone thinks differently. That's why different tactics and nuances are thrown in to help any type of learner or thinker. Stick with the base ideas and feel free to adjust and add your own twist to them that best suits you.

CHAPTER 5

GO TO CLASS

During my last years of college, I started to ask others if they needed help studying to help them improve on tests. I started offering tutor sessions to help my classmates understand the class material. This was the best way I could help them study for tests. When I was assisting my fellow students, the first thing I asked them was, "Do you attend class?"

You would be surprised by the number of people who sought my help yet had missed significant class time. I still offered as much help as I could. Despite this, they still didn't get the "boost" they were hoping for. The method of studying I'm presenting in this book isn't a magical cheat code. There's no method out there that will substitute for class attendance. Attending class is pivotal to success in college and is the first step in the process.

A strong positive correlation exists between class attendance and class performance. This means the more you go to class, the better grades you'll get. Most of the time, the professor actually includes class attendance in the final grade. Essentially, attending class is a grade booster in itself. There should be few excuses for missing class. I understand that emergencies may happen that will prevent you from going to class. These should be rare occurrences.

One point I always try to emphasize is that the college tuition is based on the classes you take. Attending college is expensive. It baffles me that someone would pay a huge price for something and not even use it or take advantage of it.

Every time a student skips class, they're throwing part of that college tuition money in the garbage. According to the Federal Reserve, around 69% of students in the class of 2018 took out student loans. The average debt balance of these loans is $29,600.[10] That's a financial commitment that should be taken seriously. Without getting into the whole "student loan crisis" debacle, attending college is expensive. Since you're spending a large amount of money to obtain a college education, you should GO TO CLASS!

While I attended college, I was friends with "honor students." Sometimes, these students took classes specifically designed for them as honor students. Since I wasn't one of these elite students, I wanted to know why they were so special. During my first couple of years at college, I got really close to one of my professors. One day, I asked the professor, "What's the main difference between your normal class and the honors class?" His answer made me realize what I had to do to be successful moving forward. He responded with a resounding, "Nothing drastic." Shocked, I asked, "What do you mean, nothing drastic?"

He then explained that the main difference is attendance and work ethic of the students. Honor classes have higher class attendance than the normal classes. They pay attention. Due to this simple fact, the professor is able to cover more material faster. Most of the students in honors classes are more regimented and focused during class. He didn't have to waste time reviewing past material. He can feel confident giving out more rigorous assignments because of this, thus, making it an honors course.

Importantly, in addition to attending class, you need to pay attention as well. I know classes can be boring at times or you may have more pressing matters on your mind. However, receiving the information that's taught in class is most important. Almost all information that will be on upcoming tests will be explained by the professor. The professor will also give practice problems or examples. These aid in the whole learning process.

The Grade-A Learning Process

I wanted to understand what it took to learn. What's the process? After reflecting on my experience, I came up with this simplified learning process. I developed this process to help college students understand what goes into learning, especially learning in the college setting. I call it the Grade-A Learning Process. To fully learn class material, you have to go through a version of this learning process. It's broken down into four phases.

The first phase is when the professor teaches on a topic and you listen, take notes, and try to learn. The professor explains all the vocabulary, definitions, reasons, and any important information. It's the background. Essentially, this is when the "why" behind the topic is explained. I call this the *listening phase.*

The second phase is when the professor demonstrates what they taught you. The professor gives examples, allegories, or practice problems. This is when the "how" or application is explained and shown. I call this the *understanding phase.*

The third phase is when the professor steps away and lets you try a problem or example on your own. This is where you apply the information you listened to and the understanding you have of it. You'll start to piece together your own solution to problems, allegories, or examples. I call this the *competence phase.*

Finally, the last step is when you feel so competent in the topic that you can teach it to someone else. You start being able to reference each topic in your own words and thoughts. I call this the *integration phase*.

THE GRADE A
learning process

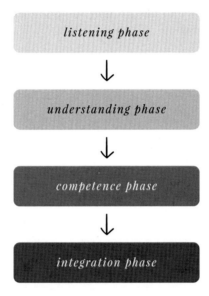

It's important to know that skipping any of these phases will make it very difficult to do well in your classes. What I came to realize is with math-based courses people tend to skip or not focus on phases 1 and 2. They tend to jump right into solving problems without having a complete understanding. They need to understand why they're solving and how to solve the problem. Some students brush past these essential parts and go right to phase 3. Frustration forms when they don't get the results they desire. Spend time and focus on these first two phases because it will make the last two, the ones you do on your own, quicker.

Of these four phases, phases 1 and 2 can only be done in the classroom. Phase 3 is either done inside and outside of the classroom. This depends on how the professor conducts their class. Phase four is done on your own or in a small group of people. Each phase is an integral part for thriving in the testing environment. Even though each phase is important in their own way, most of the phases are done in the actual classroom so... GO TO CLASS!

Your Most Valuable Resource

When I go to the movies or a show, the first thing I do is try to get the best seat in the house. I want to be able to hear and see everything perfectly. The same should apply to your college classes. Sit in a good seat, I suggest somewhere in the middle of the first couple rows of the classroom. Treat it like you're going to the movies. This way, you'll have a good view of the professor to see everything they do. In a good range to hear the professor with no problem so you can listen to everything they say. And the professor can see you as well so they can interact with you to help you whenever it's needed.

It might sound weird but having the professor see you "front and center" will give you an advantage. Be engaged in class. If, at any point, you're confused, ask questions. If you need something explained better, ask questions. If you need another example, ask questions. Develop a rapport with the professors; they're there to help you.

Professors are human just like you and me. Their career is focused on helping students understand the knowledge they're teaching. Take advantage of their office hours. They have them in case you need additional help understanding any class material. If students put in the effort, most professors will go above expectations to help them. Be teachable, be recognizable. Come every day and sit in that good seat. Also, don't be rude or distracting during class. There's nothing ruder to a professor than students who don't pay attention, especially if they're on their phones, laptops, or listening to music. Respect your professors and their time. Put away the technology and pay attention. Most importantly, GO TO CLASS!

Professors are experts in what they teach. That's why they're paid well. A college is a place where a group of highly skilled and knowledgeable teachers are gathered. Their job is to teach aspiring adults. That's the whole allure of college. What these professors say is important and should be documented. That's why taking notes is significant.

The professors in most college courses have a strong understanding of the tests that they give. What questions they will ask. The topics that will be covered. They'll make sure they teach most of the information that's on their test. So, you should write down what's taught in the classroom in order to ace upcoming tests. They are giving you the answers! Taking notes can be challenging at times. A lot of information is presented in a short amount of time. Fear not; you don't have to fully understand the information to take notes. This is the start of the Grade-A Learning Process or phase 1. The only guidelines I like to give about taking notes is that they have to be handwritten and legible.

In addition to taking notes, it's important to also pay attention to how they say it as well. Every so often, the professor will spend a suspicious amount of time on a specific topic. It's obvious that the professor thinks this topic is important. In such a case, I would put a star in my notebook next to the notes, identifying the importance of that topic. I would also put a star next to the points that the professor repeats multiple times. Also, if the professor slows down and puts a strong emphasis on a point as well. This will help me put emphasis when reviewing my notes.

As I stated earlier, professors want the students who pay attention to succeed. They'll give the students little nuggets like these to help them do that. Look out for phrases such as "Listen to me…," "This is important…," "It's important you understand…," "Again…," "I repeat…," or my favorite, "This will be on the test." I made each class sort of a game to find out what the professor was hinting at. I wanted to know what to focus on while studying in order to ace the tests and, ultimately, ace the class.

Finally, I always tended to write my notes by hand. There's something about handwriting notes that makes it superior over typing notes. A study, published in *Psychological Science*, analyzed handwriting and typing notes. Students who wrote their notes had improved learning and retention versus those who typed their notes. The study consisted of two groups of students with similar abilities. One group had to type their notes and another group had to handwrite their notes. The result showed that the students who handwritten notes had superior test scores.

After analyzing the data, a couple of reasons for these results are obvious. First of all, laptops and tablets are more distracting. Laptops can be used for many purposes other than typing. Internet access and social media platforms can sidetrack a student. Secondly, and most importantly, most people are slower at handwriting notes. This causes them to be more selective in note taking.[11]

Being selective in taking notes may seem like a negative. Selectivity causes more analyzing and processing than recording words verbatim. The brain is more active during note taking and information gathering. This results in an improvement of learning and retention. Spontaneous summarizing and paraphrasing will be a common theme in the upcoming steps. It's the scientific evidence for the success of this studying process. Nevertheless, it doesn't matter how you study if you aren't present in the classroom, so GO TO CLASS!

Chapter 5 Summary

- The more you go to class, the more success you'll have.
- College is expensive. You're paying for the classes, so make the payments worth it.
- The Grade-A Learning Process is broken up into four phases:
    o Listening, Understanding, Competence, and Integration.
    o Most of these phases are done within the classroom.
- When attending class, get a good seat upfront.
- Pay attention during class, so put the phones and laptops away.
- Professors are paid to teach and help you; they're a valuable resource.
- Take handwritten notes during class.
    o Pay attention to "important information" and acknowledge it in your notes.
- GO TO CLASS!

CHAPTER 6

OUTLINE THE TEXTBOOK

Freshman year of college was difficult for me. I was new to the dynamics of college. I was uncomfortable and intimidated. One of the first things I did was meet with a student counselor at our university's Center for Student Progress or CSP for short. The CSP's goal was to help guide students to be on the right path to succeed in college. They would advise students on all resources available to help with college coursework. They also helped set personal goals for students for their upcoming freshman year.

When I signed up for CSP's services, I was assigned Katie as my mentor. Katie had an infectious bubbly personality. Just her saying, "Hi" made you smile and bring joy to your day. At first, I was skeptical when I found out that Katie was only two years older than me. I thought to myself, *How much more experience and knowledge does she have?* When the day of my appointment arrived, I moseyed to the CSP office and into Katies cubicle.

As soon as Katie saw me walk into her cubicle, she gave me a big bright greeting, "Good Morning, Brad! How are you today?" Still skeptical of this whole situation, I gave a half-assed greeting back. After some brief small talk, Katie proceeded to get down to business. "The first thing I like to do is set a goal for your freshman year of college. What GPA do you want to achieve by the end of your second semester?"

I slowly pulled out my class schedule. I went down each class title one by one. I came up with an arbitrary grade that I would feel confident getting and wrote it next to the class. Calculating the results, I said, "I would be happy if I got a 3.6."

She wrote 3.6 down on a piece of paper and then stared at me for a few seconds. After this long awkward pause, she asked how I felt about that GPA. I confidently said that I could do this. She then erased that 3.6 and put down a frightening 4.0, which caused me to be confused and my anxiety levels to rise.

"Whoa!" I said with my eyes wide open and heart pounding, "I don't think I can achieve that! First, I don't believe I have the ability to get all A's. Secondly, if you didn't know, I'm a student athlete and I won't have the time to get a 4.0."

With a chuckle, she said, "I could see that the 3.6 goal wasn't big enough for you. If your goal doesn't scare you, then it's not big enough."

She tried to convince me to get me on board with this 4.0 GPA goal. That's when I asked, "What's the one thing I have to do to have the best shot at achieving a 4.0?"

She stopped, stared at me for a few more seconds, and said, "Do what the professor tells you to do. That means all the assignments, problems, and readings. Do them all, and you'll be fine."

As the semester progressed, I started to do just that. I would try to do everything each professor told us to do. This diligence resulted in me being on track to getting that 4.0 for the first semester of college.

That advice Katie gave me made a difference. Doing all the assignments, homework, and practice problems helped tremendously. Although, reading the textbook was tough. Textbooks are intimidating. They're long and dry. I would find out what chapter was assigned then read a couple of pages. Then I realized that I had no clue what I had just read, so I would go back and reread everything again. I realized that it was a huge waste of my time, so I stopped reading them. One month remained in the semester, and I refused to open another textbook. My grades had dropped a little in percentage; however, I still was able to maintain my straight As.

The next semester rolled around, and I was confident that I could still keep this 4.0 alive. But I had a problem: This was the start of my first college baseball season. College athletics are intense. Multiple hours are spent every day practicing and training. It's identical to working a job while taking on a full slate of classes.

On top of that, the college baseball schedule is long. The traveling is crazy, especially for a school in northeast Ohio. An average division 1 college baseball season has around 60 games. The season stretches from mid-February to mid-May. Less than a third of the games are at home. I ended up missing a decent number of classes. This put a strain on me fulfilling the student part of "student-athlete."

I began to struggle because I wasn't getting all the course material I needed from class. The only other way to receive course material was through the textbook. This created a dilemma because I knew that reading the textbook was a waste of time for me. I was in a predicament.

The first couple weeks into baseball season, I was struggling. I knew there had to be a better way to use the textbook. After scanning multiple textbooks, I developed a way to extract useful information without reading the textbook word for word. I was able to save boatloads of time while retaining and learning new material for my tests.

The method extracts information from textbooks without formal reading, then organizes that information in a way that's simple to read. This method is what I attribute my ability to maintain my perfect grades.

Reading entire textbooks is a huge waste of time, spending hours reading, rereading, and understanding the material. More effective ways to study are available instead of reading a textbook. The value added doesn't justify the time spent.

STUDYING *in college*

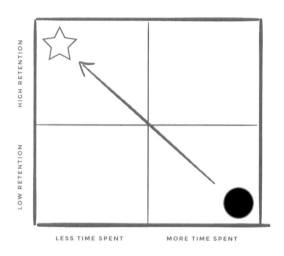

Time is valuable. To illustrate my point, look at the chart presented above. The x-axis is time spent and the y-axis is the amount of retention. You want to spend most of your time in the top left quadrant of this chart. Reading textbooks, word for word, puts you in that bottom right. The time spent reading a textbook doesn't give the amount of impact it should.

Before you turn into a student rebel and throw away all your textbooks, keep in mind that textbooks still serve an important purpose. You still need to purchase and use textbooks to have the best chance for success.

A common misconception is that textbooks are learning tools. This is one of the reasons why professors assign readings of the textbook chapters. This may cause some students to think they have to read the textbook to get the best grade on tests.

This is simply not the case. Textbooks are *reference tools*. Textbooks should be used as *supplementary material*, not the primary way to learn a topic. It's a quick look-up, reference guide to solidify information already taught to you.

For example, let's say you go on a date and you're super interested in this person. Naturally, you want to make a good first impression. You gathered some intel from friends, and you know that the person adores the Jonas Brothers. The problem is that you don't know anything about them. You proceed to go online and google "Jonas Brothers." You see the Wikipedia page regarding this topic and click on it.

I doubt that you would want to spend a lot of your time reading the whole Jonas Brothers Wikipedia page. Instead, you quickly read the introduction. Look through the main topics of the page and skim the most prevalent topics. You do this to get the most important information that will "wow" your date. On one hand, you don't want to spend too much time reading about this specific topic. On the other hand, you know that some of the information is important to grasp. That's how you use textbooks in college.

The point of this step is to skim textbooks, like you would a Wikipedia page. Pull out the most important info and write it down in outline form. This step is important because it's the start of the integration phase of the Grade-A Learning Process. Before doing the skimming process, it's important to understand an outline. What it is and how it's used. An outline is a way to present the main points or topics of a given subject. The points are organized in a way to show hierarchical relationships among the points. The hierarchical relationships are shown through indentations. A point that's indented gives a more in-depth explanation to the topic(s) or point(s) above it. This outline structure is used in the summary at the end of each chapter in this book.

Below is an example of the structure of an outline. Understanding this is important in order to move on in the studying process. If you have any confusion about outlines, please take the time to understand them. Knowing outlines, their purpose, and structure is important before moving on.

Main Topic

> Main Point #1
>> Supporting Point # 1 for Main Point # 1
>>> Example/supporting info
>> Supporting Point # 2 for Main Point # 1
> Main Point #2
>> Supporting Point # 1 for Main Point # 2
>> Supporting Point # 2 for Main Point # 2
>>> Example/supporting info
>>> Example/supporting info
>> Supporting Point # 3 for Main Point # 2
> Main Point #3
>> Supporting Point # 1 for Main Point # 3
>> Supporting Point # 2 for Main Point # 3

Side Note: Outlining is also used to aid in writing papers. It also helps with giving speeches, presentations, or talks.

The point of any book is to pass along a core idea to inform or better the audience. Books break down this core idea with a series of chapters or main points. This helps the audience understand the core idea better. In each chapter, the author will break down the material even further into subtopics. These subtopics have information pertaining to that chapter and the core idea. The subtopics can even be condensed further into supporting details. These are usually examples portrayed through analogies, stories, or supporting research.

Textbooks, and almost every non-fiction book, are just expanded outlines. The goal of this outlining step is to pull out the main points you think the author is trying to make, disregarding all the supporting details. The additional words, phrases, unnecessary information, research, and examples can be left out.

To simplify outlining the textbook, the objective is to go into the mind of the author. What are the most important points you want to make? Essentially, you'll be reverse engineering the book back into its original format. This is the format that the author had to use to start writing the textbook. Importantly, remember to only include main topics and subtopics. I want to overemphasize the following points. Throw out all the supporting examples you've heard in class and create your own. Disregard research that the author used to back up the information. I think we can all trust that they did their due diligence and the research is correct. Forget any fillers used in the textbook to create length. These will only waste your time and demand more effort.

This might seem like a daunting task, but most textbooks are designed to make this super easy. All headings and subheadings are usually bolded and/or underlined. You can pick these out almost immediately while leafing through a textbook. The meat of the information is usually in these subsections. Pulling out what's important usually takes minimal effort. All the important information and points the author is trying to make are either bolded, italicized, or in a list.

Bold text is used to highlight keywords. It lends an emphasis to these specific words/phrases. Italics are used for a very similar reason: to bring notice to that word or phrase. Treat textbooks like you would a professor teaching a class. As mentioned in the "Go to Class" step, the professor will use certain nuances to bring attention to a specific idea, repeat it, put emphasis on it, or say, "Pay attention, this is important." The bolding and italicizing of text are the literal forms of this in a textbook.

There's also another tip to get a better understanding of a topic while skimming a textbook. The first and last couple of sentences of each section are usually summaries. Authors tend to hint at what they're going to tell you in the beginning of a section. They also will give a summary of what they explained at the end. Skim those first and last sentences to get that quick summary.

While creating this outline, write down the information by hand. Grammar, proper spelling, and full sentences don't matter. This is where you can save the most time studying and have the best retention. The brain will have a better opportunity to learn when information is analyzed. While skimming, analyze the points to figure out what's the most important part of each sentence. Copying anything verbatim doesn't help with long-term retention. This should be taken out of your student practices.

While you do this outline phase, I want you to take the summarizing and paraphrasing to the maximum. The fewer full words, the better. Use abbreviations and even symbols to portray various words. For example, I'm going to summarize and paraphrase the previous couple sentences. If I wanted to include these sentences in my outline, it would look something like the following. (Outline: summ/para ↑↑↑, < words = better, words → abbrv. & symb.) Go crazy with it.

I use a lot of arrows when writing my notes/outlines. How I draw the arrow means different things. For example, when I use the up arrow this means "enhances," "increases," or "improves." A down arrow means "decreases" or "reduces." An arrow pointing to the right means to me leads to, turn into, resulting in, etc. An arrow with an arch, ⌢, means something completely different. An arrow that has a squiggly line, ⤳, another meaning entirely.

Whatever you decide doesn't matter, as long as you can understand your shorthand is the point. Breaking down sentences is a way to trigger the information that's already in your brain. Full sentences present the information without the brain doing too much work. Getting to the final product of this condensed outline matters and helps with maximizing studying.

Finally, as an added bonus, I found it helpful to put page numbers of the textbook throughout my outline. This will help you to reference the textbook for certain occasions. For instance, this is helpful if you happen to forget the meaning of a point in your outline. Sometimes you might break down a point so much that you can't recall the meaning. You can then quickly turn back to the exact page you got that information to understand what you meant. Also, this helps tremendously with open-book and -note tests.

Open-book and -note tests are usually traps for most students. With these tests, it's natural to think you need to do little to no preparation to ace them. That's 100% wrong. Open-book and -note tests are usually created in a way to make it difficult to use the references. If you use the textbook for most of the questions, you won't have time to finish. By doing these outlines you're already retaining information pertaining to the tests. Plus, you also have a quick page reference guide if you need to look back into the textbook.

To summarize: Scan each chapter. Pull out the relevant information (headings, subheadings, bolded/italicized items, and lists). Write it down in outline form, and don't use full sentences. Even though this step requires the most amount of "work," doing this will save you the most time. It will also give you the most retention and set you up for success.

Chapter 6 Summary

- Textbooks are valuable reference tools, not learning tools.
- A lot of time is wasted reading textbooks word for word.
- Outline the textbook information by hand:
    o Extract important information in textbooks through skimming.
    o Don't use full sentences or proper grammar.
    o Get into the mind of the author and find points the author is trying to make.
    o Periodically put page numbers as references.
- These outlines are great for open-book and -note tests.

COMBINE NOTES AND OUTLINE

College taught me an abundance of lessons that I've applied to my professional career. A topic that stands out in particular is a concept from my business management course called "synergy." Synergy is the combination of two or more people, groups, or things to produce a combined effect that's greater than the sum of their separate effects. The additional value is added when two or more things work together in harmony.

A simple illustration for synergy is 1+1=3. A well-formed team can get more done than many people working individually. When things that are meant for each other are combined, it generates a multiplying power. The benefits of synergy are real and should be taken advantage of.

A lot of real-life examples pertaining to the power of synergy can be found. We see this a lot in the food industry with new recipes being created every day. The Internet is riddled with food-related questions regarding recipes. People want to know what they can add to a specific dish to make it taste better as a whole. What works well together and what doesn't. What complements a certain ingredient or dish and what do you want to avoid. The Food Network has made a fortune on this fascination with food combinations.

A guilty pleasure of mine was watching the shows starring either Guy Ferrari or Gordon Ramsay. I realized that when either one tried a meal they liked, they would use specific words and phrases. They were so vivid when trying to illustrate the greatness of the dish. They would describe certain ingredients or flavors and how they worked to add value to the dish as a whole. Words like "complemented," "boosted," "adds," "blends," "works with," and "crafted" are a few. These words were used to describe synergy among the ingredients.

Eating the ingredients separately gives a contrasting experience than eating them cooked together. The combination of ingredients is a flavorful example of how synergy works in the real world.

As a kid, I always wanted to experiment to create new adventures for myself. It started off small with simple sandwiches. Peanut butter and jelly sandwiches were great. Peanut butter and banana were amazing. Peanut butter and marshmallow fluff, my mind was blown.

Food was the beginning of my wanting to create, combine. I started playing with Play-Doh and LEGO, making jumbled messes. But, to me, they were works of art. Whatever I played with, I tried to make better than the last.

I've been on sports teams and school project groups where everything just clicked. We were able to build on and complement each other. The different perspectives among our teammates widen our view. We understood the complete picture of what exactly we had to do to reach our goals.

A full spectrum of possibilities is available once synergy is tapped. You'll always stand taller with someone on your shoulders. All these are real-life examples of how synergy is all around us from childhood to adulthood. Find ways to add value, complement, and improve whatever you're doing. This also applies to improving current studying practices.

As college students you have access to two main information sources for your classes. These main sources are your textbook and your professor. You also have auxiliary sources in your peers and real-life examples. All this info can be combined into one item, something clear and distinct, one item to answer all your questions and covers all your studying needs. It's time to unlock the power of studying synergy.

After attending class, you should have a notebook filled with notes from class. After outlining the textbook, you should have a written outline. Both of these presents you with all the information needed for your next test. Now take out a couple of fresh sheets of paper and combine your class notes with the outline. This will create a single document with all the information you need to succeed for your tests.

Essentially, you'll be rewriting your textbook outline and inserting your class notes. Be cognizant of putting your notes under the correct headings that pertain to each point. Combining your class notes and your textbook outline will make a synergistic document. Since you're using your notes and your outline, this has your personal touch.

Once you start, you'll begin to realize a lot of overlapping information. Obviously, the professor mentioned similar content to the textbook and vice versa. If the notes are almost identical to the outline of the textbook, then you won't be adding too much to the outline. Sometimes, though, professors will go rogue in their class and have their own flow. They'll be bouncing back and forth between chapters and topics. This could make for confusing and unproductive studying. Although this may get a little tricky, inserting the notes into the textbook outline is best.

Textbooks are methodically planned and organized. They're written with a flow that makes sense for the readers to get information in the best way. Use the textbook's organizational scheme, it will be the most beneficial.

During this phase, make sure you copy over all the attention getters. These are the stars, circles, and underlines that you put into your notes.

If you remember, these attention getters are for points that the professor emphasized. That way, you can still have those hints and still focus on those points moving forward.

Finally, keep on trying to condense the information you put into this new outline. Using more abbreviations and symbols and less words/phrases. Break them down as much as possible. Make it easy on yourself. The fewer words you write, the more time you save. The goal of this step is to have all information in one document. If you have this master outline completed, move on to the next step: Rewrite and Condense.

Chapter 7 Summary

- Synergy is when the combined effect is greater than the sum of the individuals.
- Make a synergistic outline by combining your class notes into your textbook outline.
- Maintain the flow of the original outline.
- Rewrite them by hand.
- Break down and clean up as much as possible:
  o Leave out repeated information.
  o Condense the information as much as possible.
  o Make it easier to rewrite.
- Keep the attention getters from original outline and class notes.

CHAPTER 8

REWRITE AND CONDENSE

I was a math kid growing up. At a very young age, I developed a fascination for mathematics. I was innately curious about understanding the purpose behind solving the problems. I loved the idea of seeing a problem and solving it. By my middle school years, I began to be talented in mathematics. I focused on grasping the definitions, vocabulary, and reasons behind math problems. Once I understood the information, I was able to apply the principles of how to solve more easily.

I spent a lot of time in the first two phases of the Grade-A Learning Process. Phase 1 where I listened to the information. Phase 2 where I developed an understanding of how to apply the information. With that time and focus on the first two phases, phases 3 and 4 came more natural and easier. To me, there was just one task: to solve. One and done.

This one and done mindset caused me to dislike writing and essays. Math problems have a completely different process on how to solve than writing an essay or paper. There's usually only one way to solve a math problem and usually only one answer. However, with writing, there are a lot of complex ideas and original thoughts. These all need to be developed and put together in a way that makes sense and is easy to follow. Don't forget about all the proper spelling, grammar, and punctuation involved. All these factors play a huge role in making a piece of writing perfect.

In my grade school years, I would get terrible grades on my essays and papers. I would write it once and turn them in, like I would with any math problem. I had so many errors in my writing that I would get knocked down several letter grades on every paper I would write. I would get comments throughout my papers pertaining to the errors I had. The flow of the paper was poor. I constantly repeated information throughout the paper. I had numerous run-on sentences, incomplete thoughts, bad spelling and grammar. The list could go on forever.

I would try to apply these comments in future papers in order to get a better grade. This caused me to work slower and more diligently. I wanted to correct these common issues I was experiencing. I was now spending a lot more time writing these papers, though to my demise, I was receiving similar results. Not until my sophomore year in high school did everything change. My writing teacher flipped my mindset and changed my writing process.

This writing class had its first paper due not too far into the semester. When we turned in the paper, the teacher called my name to stay after class to talk to her. I began mentally scrolling through the gauntlet of things I may have been in trouble for. After not coming up with anything, I moseyed over to her.

She plopped my paper down on the desk, which had a fiesta of red pen markings on it. I slouched over her desk while looking at the paper as she began to question my writing process. I mumbled a phrase which can be summarized into "I just wrote it." Letting out a sigh, she said, "Look, against my better judgement, I'm going to give you another shot at this. Do you still have this paper saved on your computer?"

I lethargically shook my head, yes. "I want you to take back your paper and treat it like your first rough draft. I need you to go through this paper and make a second rough draft. Focus on the paper organization, the flow, and transitions. After that second rough draft, I want you to edit it multiple times for spelling and grammar. If you can get a peer to edit it after, that would be an added bonus. When you're done with that, turn it in."

Subtly rolling my eyes, I acknowledged her suggestion and left. I spent a couple days rereading and editing. I realized the paper was getting better through each of these phases. Each following step in this writing process took less time than the prior. By the end, I was amazed by how much better the paper seemed. Pride filled my body when I completed this paper. I strolled into class and placed my paper on the teacher's desk.

The next day, she passed back all the papers to the class. When she placed my freshly done paper, my eyes widened in disbelief. An A! I never received an A on a paper before. In the corner she wrote, "I expect nothing less from you moving forward. Nothing is great the first time you do it. USE THE WRITING PROCESS!" My attitude changed that day. Revising and editing were essential parts of the writing process. I couldn't shortcut those if I cared about being successful.

For example, if I had published the first rough draft of this book's manuscript, you would have thrown it away by now. This manuscript has been through many rounds of revising and editing to polish it into what it is now. I did a second rough draft, many rounds of self-editing and a verbal read through. The manuscript went through editing software, peer reviews, and professional editing. Each step made my book better and better until it became this polished version of what you see today.

I found out that redoing and refining also applies to much more than writing a paper or a book. Anything, besides your basic rudimentary tasks, can benefit from analyzing and correcting. You can always make something better. That's where this next method of studying and learning comes into play.

Rewriting and condensing can polish your outline into the best studying tool. This is an important step for your larger tests and complex class material. I find that it helps with classes with an abundance of information. The value of this may decrease if the outline is already small or material isn't too difficult.

If this is the case, the next step may seem repetitive and pointless. The repetitive nature is what helps with integration and retention. Embrace the repetition. Repetition is a powerful tool that can be used to your advantage. If your outline is lengthy with loads of information, then this step is necessary. Now before you skip rewriting your outline, it's important to review your outline. Get a complete understanding of what needs to be rewritten and what doesn't. This knowledge only comes through experience. Rewriting and condensing your outline has importance. It can make a big difference in your test performance. Take the time and find out what this process entails. Then you can decide if this step is necessary or not. Personally, I rewrote every one of my outlines. I may have not condensed them, but the repetition helped me.

I would like to mention a couple of points that will make this process easier. First, make sure no information is repeated. If so, only rewrite that information once on the new outline. Next, if any information is what you would consider "duh" information, throw it out. "Duh" information is obvious or what you already know. It's integrated. It's something you look at and automatically think, *Yeah, I know this in my sleep* or *That's common sense.* Throw out any information that you know already because it doesn't hold any more importance. If you already know it and it's already instilled into your brain, then there's no point in rewriting it. This is the ultimate way to condense the outline.

It's important to make this outline aesthetically appealing (i.e., make it look good). There's a common phrase in sports: "Look good, feel good, play good." Growing up, I played on a travel baseball team called the Mahoning Valley Venom from 8 to 12 years old. In those five years, we won a considerable number of games and tournaments. One of them being the USSSA World Series, when we were 10 years old.

At the beginning of every baseball year, we took weeks designing our perfect jersey. We needed everyone on our team to think they were sweet. The jerseys needed to have swag. Every year when we got these new jerseys, we felt like we were in the pros. I would just put that jersey on and wear it around the house. My family used to catch me staring at myself in the mirror trying to figure out what was the best way to wear my jersey. How many buttons should be undone? Should I wear my pant legs up or down? How much jersey do I tuck in? Should my hat brim be flatter or curved and by how much?

This may seem silly to you but when I stepped onto that field, I felt like a million bucks. I assume that my teammates did as well because we were a good little team back then. We may have been young; nevertheless, we had some swagger wearing those uniforms. We were intimidating to opposing teams. We knew we looked good, we knew we felt good, and, boy oh boy, did we play good.

When you rewrite that outline, make sure you like how it looks and that you feel good about it. Be proud of it. If the outline looks good, and if you feel good about it, you'll test well. A good rule of thumb is that each chapter's outline should be averaging one-and-a-half to two pages. That's not saying you can't have more or less, it's an average to have that size for the average textbook chapter. Use it as a benchmark.

What I like to do after I'm done rewriting my outline is to put it next to the textbook and see the difference in size. It's an accomplishment to get to this point. You can physically see the breakdown of a textbook into a short outline. The goal at this point is to have a new polished outline. Rewrite and/or condense it into something more appealing and manageable. Once you have that, it's time for the final step: Read and Teach.

Chapter 8 Summary

- Rewriting your current outline will help refine and ingrain the information.
  - o The repetition of writing the information is a good thing; it helps with memorization.
- Throw out any points and notes that aren't necessary:
  - o Repeated information
  - o Information that you already know in your sleep
- Make your outline's size manageable.
- Make your outline aesthetically pleasing; make it look good.
- Usually you'll finish with an outline consisting of a couple pages per chapter.

READ AND TEACH

I'm always fascinated with the concept of having something be second nature to you. It's intriguing to have a particular characteristic, skill, or habit become instinctual. These are ingrained in your mind because you've behaved in a particular way often. Repeating the same thing the same way imbeds this function into your mind.

Transitioning from your conscious mind to your unconscious mind creates these habits. This transition is what creates this phenomenon of second nature, obtaining knowledge through your unconscious mind and applying it to actions. In other words, your mind is going on autopilot.

Everyone has experienced this, usually in their childhood. It often starts with the repetition of a specific action, causing those actions to be ingrained in their brains. When they attempt to do the action again, they can do it without thinking. Riding a bike, swimming, and throwing a ball are all examples of this. Let's say a boy learned how to ride a bike. He would ride that bike many times throughout his childhood. Now that same kid grew up and doesn't ride a bike anymore. Do you think that as an adult, he'll need to go through a step-by-step process to achieve this task again? No, the information that's necessary to achieve riding a bike is rooted deep within his mind. He can recall that information in a moment's notice without any complex thinking.

When I was around five years old, I was obsessed with LEGOs. I would play with them constantly and always wanted to build something new. I spent multiple hours, even days, figuring out how to build whatever I wanted to create.

One time, when I was eight years old, I was running around my basement, like all kids do. No shoes or socks on. I was carefree. I then stepped on one of those iconic yellow LEGO minifigure. The pain radiated through my whole body and caused me to drop to my knees. I spent the next couple seconds screaming due to the immense pain in my foot. When the pain dissipated, I said to myself, "If only these LEGO men were bigger, I could see them and not step on them."

An idea immediately popped up in my head to build a bigger LEGO man using LEGOs. After weeks and weeks of building, I built a two-foot-tall replica of the LEGO minifigure. I was so proud of myself when I finished; I showed it to my parents. Their raised eyebrows and slight head nod showed they were so impressed.

They asked me, "How did you manage to do something like this?" I thought hard and the only thing I could think of was, "I don't know; I just did it."

My parents began to buy complex LEGO kits meant for adults 18 and over. I was able to build every one of them: the Statue of Liberty, a giant dinosaur, Yoda, Cinderella's castle, the Eiffel Tower, the list goes on. Building these LEGO creations became so effortless. I found it hard to explain to people how I actually built them. The methods I use and the way I thought were second nature to me. I became a natural at building LEGOs after years of practice and repeated building. I could instantly pick up where I left off and had a solution to any problem I experienced in a moment's notice. Playing with LEGOs was now my second nature.

When I was older, I wanted to make studying at the macro and micro levels second nature as well. I had a goal to find the best way of studying. I tried many different methods. Periodically adding nuances throughout my studying process. I repeated the same process with everything I needed to study until it was instinctive for me to study the most important things.

During college, some of my colleagues asked me, "How do you maintain your good grades while having such an active lifestyle?" At first, I didn't know how to answer. My humility kicked in and I gave the stereotypical answer of, "I don't know, I'm just lucky I guess." After hearing that question several times, I decided I needed to find the answer. I took the time and reflected on the true reason why. I made choices, followed processes in order to maximize my studying and do well on tests. Luck wasn't involved at all. The ways I prepared and studied are what got me to this high level of achievement. I also realized the amount of precise repetition I did helped me a lot. This repetition embeds information into my mind. It's also one of the premises of this studying method and is the last step.

Read Through Your Outline

Start by reading your final outline from beginning to end. Repeat. Read it over multiple times. It shouldn't take long to do because this outline is condensed. After going over the outline a couple times, you'll realize you're starting to memorize it. You start recalling what the next point is going to be before you even get there. When you realize this, start covering up the next line of the outline with another paper. This will test you to see if you have memorized your outline. Once you can recall your whole outline from memory, you're practically ready for the test.

Memorizing can be hard for people, so I've found some tricks to help with this task. The use of different colors or symbols helps with memory. These will bring attention and differentiation to specific pieces of information. This helps the brain recall areas that you're having a difficult time remembering.

For instance, if you get to a point where you can't recall a specific topic, highlight or circle the key word in the point. After any additional time that you read it and recollection still isn't there, use different colors or symbols (underlines, boxes, triangles, cloud shapes, etc.). Come up with any system you like. Using colors and symbols will add more visual stimuli. This will help with memorizing and retention.

For example, I would read my master outline three times. After the third time, I would start covering up the outline and go line by line trying to recall it. Whenever I would miss or get caught up on a point, I would highlight a keyword. After going through the whole outline, I would then repeat the same process. This time, if I forgot anything, I would underline the keyword I couldn't recall. Finally, if I go through one more round and still can't remember a specific topic. I would then draw a box around the keyword of that topic. Now there are colors and symbols throughout the outline. I would now recall this information better with all these visual stimuli.

Another strategy I've used is acronyms or wacky sentences. This usually works best when trying to memorize lists. Acronyms are words formed by abbreviating the first letter of each word. For example, NASA stands for National Aeronautics and Space Administration.

There will be instances where the first letters of words don't form a coherent, easy to pronounce word. When that happens then come up with a whacky sentence using the first letters.

A common example is the planets: MVEMJSUNP. Now that specific acronym is impossible to say as a single word. This resulted in the creation of a wacky sentence to help memorization. My Very Educated Mother Just Served Us Nine Pizzas. (Many variations for this acronym exist. This is the sentence that I learned.) Mercury, Venus, Earth, Mars, Jupiter, Saturn, Uranus, Neptune, Pluto. (I have no idea if they still technically consider

Pluto as a planet or not, but I still do because that's how I learned it). The more whacky, crazy, and visually engaging the sentence is the easier it's to remember.

The brain is very fascinating. There are tricks you can do that can improve the brain's ability to memorize, retain, and recall information. I realized while studying that the more senses I used, the more information I retained. Also, the less time it took to ingrain the information into my brain.

The better you are at combining visual and auditory information, the better retention. This conclusion was reached by neuroscientists at the University of Lausanne in Switzerland. They demonstrated the effectiveness of teaching methods that simultaneously use multiple senses.[12] Now, most studies only focus on two of the five senses: auditory/hearing and visual/seeing.

When I study, I try to use all five senses to activate my brain. The results give me an easier time retaining the information. Now before you think I'm crazy, I'm not going to say you have to lick and smell your notes or books, unless you want to; to each their own. However, a tactic I used for smell was that I burned a candle next to me while studying. Pick a scent that's unique, that you like. I also chewed peppermint gum while studying. I also have mints available that I routinely eat and have easy access to. Bring the gum and the scent you used for studying to the test. It will help with recall when you experience those unique scents again.

For touch, I would quickly tap the center of my forehead. I did this when having a difficult time remembering certain bits of information. This location on my forehead actually has some cultural relevance. It's known in Hinduism to be your "third eye" and a gateway to your soul and essence. It also symbolizes a state of enlightenment. When tapping this location, I would imagine my mind absorbing the information.

For hearing, I would sometimes softly play music, mainly instrumentals or songs with limited lyrics. For example, in the background, I would play classical music or relaxing tones that you would find in a spa. Also, I found it helpful to say my outline out loud when reading it so I could hear the information along with seeing it. When talking through your outline, visualize yourself teaching it to someone else. This helps with auditory engagement. Also, it makes your brain transition the information into a teachable format.

Finally, for seeing, you have your outline. This outline has symbols, shapes, and colors to make it more visually unique and appealing. The more senses you get involved, the more neurons will fire in your brain, making it more active in the learning and studying process.

The brain is a complex organ. Countless hours of research have been conducted trying to understand the organ, how it works and operates. One aspect is the brain's short- and long-term memory process. Researchers attest that memories are scattered across the brain's sensory centers. They're then gathered and grouped together by a region in the brain called the hippocampus. The hippocampus is a small area of the brain which regulates motivation, emotion, learning, and memory.[13]

With having a growth mindset, you want to have the ability to strengthen and access this region of the brain. Our ability to learn and remember facts and events is called declarative memory. Declarative memory happens when large networks in the brain work with the hippocampus. For memories to be long-term, even more areas of the brain are needed. Long-term memory requires more areas to fire, encode, and retrieve information. This includes visual images, sounds, words, and different sensorial occurrences.

I don't want to go too deep into the anatomy and physiology of the brain because that's a rabbit hole I don't want to explore. The big picture is that the five human senses are tied to memory gathering and access. The more stimuli the brain gets, the more activity it experiences. The more distinct and unique the sensorial experiences, the more likely you can activate the learning and memory centers. The brain will be able to access the information easier and faster.

Everyone's brain is unique. Everyone's brain will be affected differently with different experiences. Experiment with different combinations of sensory items while you study. Find out what works best and stick to it. It's not brain science.

Teach the Information

The second part of this chapter is to teach the material you're studying. If you can recall, this was already mentioned when talking about the Grade-A Learning Process. To reiterate, phase one is listening. Phase two is understanding. Phase three is competency. The final phase is integration. This involves being competent enough to teach the information to someone else. It's important that you already have an acceptable understanding of the material. This is needed before studying with other people. People can have different interpretations. They can try to persuade you into their way of thinking. This can possibly confuse you if you don't have a certain level of competence. Keep this in mind while in group studying sessions. Be aware of the interactions that are happening.

When I get to this step, I usually have a small group of people I study with, my "A-Team." An "A-Team" is a group of elite people or your top advisers whom you have surrounded yourself with. This concept was mentioned in The Master's Environment chapter of this book. This is where having a supportive group of friends or colleagues benefits you the most. They'll boost your chances at academic success. If you don't have an A-Team then try to meet up with someone in your class. Talk with them about the information to get clarity and make sure everyone is on the same page. Basically, trying to summarize what everyone thinks could be on the upcoming test.

If you're wrong on something or you don't know a topic, then ask for help. With new information, go through the four phases of the Grade-A Learning Process. Listen to the person explaining it. Then have them apply the information or do a practice problem. After that, try to give your own example or attempt another problem. Finally, explain the information like you're teaching them.

I always had a desire to help someone succeed. I always felt joyful when I could help people with academics. When someone asked for my help in a class, I almost always accepted. I also knew helping them would help me as well. It's a win-win scenario. Say yes when people ask you for help because they're helping you as well. Also, never be afraid to ask someone else for help. It's a win-win scenario for everyone involved. Everyone is getting value.

What if you don't feel comfortable with meeting new people or studying in a group? Don't worry; there's always a plan B. To all the loners out there, pretend like you're explaining the material to someone. Create an invisible friend. Grab your pet and teach them. Use a giant white board and pretend like you're teaching a class on the subject. Whatever method you use, make sure it involves auditory teaching and explaining.

Although having another human was the best method for me, it isn't the only option. The overall goal of this step is to read your outline enough times that you memorize it. Then have the ability to teach the information to someone else. If you achieve this, then you're ready to go for your test and kick some butt doing so. Good luck!

Chapter 9 Summary

- Read the outline multiple times until you can start to anticipate the next point.
  - o Repetition is the point; it's what fuels the integration process.
- Try to read outline through memory; if having difficulty, use the following:
  - o Use colors and symbols.
  - o Use acronyms.
  - o Use wacky sentences, the crazier and more visual the better.
- While studying, incorporate as many of your senses as possible.
- Grab a group of friends or someone who needs help and teach the material to them.
  - o Studying in a group has numerous benefits.
  - o If having difficulty, talk it out loud as if you're teaching it to a group.

CONCLUSION

Congratulations! You have just progressed through the methods to move you from stress to success. This will help you save time, simplify studying, and ace your college experience. You'll now be more likely to learn and retain information to ace your classes. Before you apply these studying methods, make sure you have a clear understanding of the *Grade-A Learning Process*. *Listening* to the information and taking notes. *Understanding* how to apply the information given. *Competency* in applying the information yourself. *Integration* of the knowledge so you could teach it to someone else. Also, know where you land on this process at any specific moment. Figure out the work you have to do to get to the next step of that process.

Once you understand that, you can move onto the meat of acing tests. *Go to class.* You need to know what the professor is teaching. *Outline your textbook.* The textbook is an important resource that needs to be used. *Combine your class notes with your outline.* This will make a synergistic document that's organized. *Condense the outline.* Making it into a document that you can easily navigate. *Read and teach the outline.* The repetition helps engrain the test material into your brain. Doing these will set you on your way to success.

Remember, you control your success. The mindset you have, the environment you create, and the work put in determines your success. No more blame game, no more helplessness. Take control of your life and step it into gear.

Finally, there's an added bonus when you use this method of studying. The master outlines that you create, SAVE THEM! If you ever need to look back at a previous topic, you have it right in front of you. You can quickly recall any important information in a blink of an eye. Also, if you keep these outlines, they're great for studying for midterms and finals.

I have saved an abundance of time and stress preparing for midterms and finals. I already have all the information through short condensed outlines. I can go straight to that last phase: read and teach and be ready for these big daunting exams in no time.

One piece I always like to add is that these outlines are non-transferable. Countless times people have asked me for my outlines or even tried to buy them from me. At first, I would let them have a copy; however, they wouldn't benefit from them. I cannot emphasize enough how many times they told me they didn't work or make sense. To reiterate, it's not the actual outline that helps you learn and retain information. The process of making the outline and how you use what you created is what helps you learn. The complete outlining process is where the learning happens. The reading and teaching of the outline are what cements the information into your brain.

This also goes the other way, you can't buy the outline or borrow from someone else, you have to do the work. At first, it may be challenging because it's new. The more persistent you are, the easier it will get and the more success you'll have. I hope this process helps you as much as it helped me.

As an added bonus I've included some of my outlines I made during college. These outlines are from my accounting and finance classes. I've included five samples of my outlines so you can see how they looked. This is just an example. You can organize your outlines in a different manner. Use whatever symbols you like. You can use colored highlighters if you so desire. Find out what works best for you and always keep searching to improve it.

Remember to set your groundwork and do the legwork. These are great tools to help you save time in your academics. You can use that time to build relationships, network, and ultimately have fun in college. College presents a great opportunity for personal development. However, it won't last forever; make it count, have fun, and make it memorable.

Examples

Example #1:

Chapter 1   Ethics

Why Important?
1. Investment/Capital Budgeting (CF, Ratios)
2. Financing (find right combo)
   · debt
   · equity

✳ Ethical = ↑ reputation
   reputation value

Management's Primary Objective
✳ - Shareholder (wealth max) → max stock price market value
   · Employment growth ↑
      - manager into owners (stock options)
   · Consumer welfare ↑
      · ↑ quality
      - like working

Aspects of Cash Flow → Investment value (3)
1. Amount (bigger)
✳ 2. Timing (sooner)
3. Risk (less)

Free Cash Flows (FCF)
↳ free for distribution to all investors
   · Revenues - Operating Costs - operating Taxes - Req. Investments in operating Capital

✳ Fundamental value
= $\frac{FCF_n}{(1 + WACC)^n}$

Weighted Average Cost of Capital (WACC)
↳ avg. rate of return required by all investors
· Factors
   - Capital structure (debt to equity)
   - Interest Rates
   - Risk
   - Investors attitude (risk)

Firm's value - $\sum FCF$ → today's $

WACC → measures risk

✳ Agency Relationship
↳ whenever 1+ individuals (principals) hires another (agent) to perform service / delegate decision-making
   Conflicts (2)   shareholders   managers   authority to them
   ✳ · b/w Stockholders and managers → too much power
      · b/w Stockholders and creditors
         · Creditor claim on EBIT (1st)
           Stockholders claim on Residual Earnings (2nd)

Problem
✳ Different Incentives
   b/w owners + managers

✳ Reduce Problems (actions)
   · Compensation ———→ · Reasonable Salary
   · threat of firing   · Cash/Stock Bonus
   · ↑ monitoring   · Stock Options
                             · Tie to Economic Value Added
                               EBIT (1-Tax) - WACC × Capital

Example #2:

Chapter 3 : International Monetary policy pg. 88

- History
- < 1921 → used gold/silver   Why gold didn't work
- Classical Gold Standard ⇒ Paper backed by gold
- Gold Exchange Standard → US + Britian held gold
- Bretton Woods System - fixed to US Dollar to gold - countries fixed to USD
- Free floating - Demand + Supply

→ - Central Bank cannot provide liquidity during financial crisis
- Cannot Print $ in gold standard

- The Trilemma of exchange rates pg. 90
  - Only have 2 of 3 - interest rate, exchange rate, + cap. Market integration
- European Union pg. 110
  - Maastricht Criteria pg. 114
  - European Monetary Union

Recession: ↓ Tax ↑ Spending stimulus
Austerity: ↑ Tax ↓ Spending

welfare → Tax Revenue , ↓ Fiscal Deficit

- Exchange Rate Systems pg. 92

Chapter 4: Parity Condition + Foreign Currency Forecasting

-Law of one price (Arbitrage) pg. 136
-Five Parity Conditions
  - PPP pg. 143 - 1 unit of currency → same purchasing power globally

$\$$Print $\$$ → ↑ inflation → recession

$$\frac{e_t}{e_0} = \frac{(1+\ddot{i}n)^6}{(1+if)^6}$$

$\ast$ Foreign on the bottom $\ast$

↑ inflation → currency ↓
Real → inflation !!

pg. 155 -Fisher Effect - real interest rate should be the same among countries $T_t → T_r$

$$(1+r) = (1+\overset{real}{a}) \ast (1+i) \quad or \quad r = a + i$$

pg. 159 International Fisher Effect

$$\bar{e}_t = e_0 \ast \frac{(1+rn)^6}{(1+rf)^6}$$

$\ast$ Carry Trade 162

Real Interest Rate

$$e'_t = e_t \frac{P_f}{P_h}$$

pg. 163 Interest Rate Parity

$$f_1 = e_0 \ast \left(\frac{1+rn}{1+rf}\right)$$

Forward Premium forward for currency = foreign

$$\frac{f}{e} \quad or \quad \frac{1+rh}{1+rf}$$

-Foreign Exchange Rate Forecasting pg. 171

Example #3:

Chapter 12 - Capital Budgeting

Estimating Incremental Cash Flows

 ↳ Δ in cash flow if project is taken
  • after-tax
  • exclude: Sunk cost - cannot be avoided if not taken
        Finance Cost - in required rate of return
  • include: Opportunity Cost - CF it'll lose by taking
       Externalities - effect on other firm's cash flows
  • timing is everything

Independent - CF are unaffected by acceptance (can accept more than 1) → If +NPV

Mutually Exclusive - CF are adversely impacted by acceptance (can only accept 1)
  ↳ capital budget limits

- NPV
 - CFj , I/YR → NPV   ↳ Assumes reinvest at r (Op. Cost) realistic
               ↳ mutually exclusive projects
 - If NPV > 0 = accept or highest NPV if mutually Exclusive

- IRR
 - CFj → IRR
 - If IRR > WACC (r) → or ↑ IRR
 - Drawbacks ① Size ② No/Multi Solutions ③ Borrowing/Lending ④ Reinvestment
                          ↳ at IRR

- MIRR
 - PV of = $\dfrac{TV \text{ or } CF}{(1 + MIRR)^n}$ → $\sum CF_B (1+ =/YR)^{n-p}$ Reinvest a WACC
   outflows
 - Assumes reinvestment a WACC   PV = NPV of outflows
 - No multiple IRR

- PI
 - $\dfrac{NPV}{C_0}$

- Payback
         when < P_n
 - $C_0 - P_1 CF - P_2 CF ... / P_n$ # # of n
 - Strengths ① Indication to risk + liquidity   ② Easy to calculate
 - Weakness ① Ignores TVM   ② Ignores CF after payback

Example #4:

Chapter 19 - Lease   ↓ debt capacity

- **Lessee** - uses asset + make the payments (financing decision)

  Lessor - owns asset + receives payments (investment decision)

- Operating Lease   ↗ ↓D
  - OFF balance sheet financing (Improve leverage ratio) → disclosed
  - Short-term (cancelable)

- Capital Lease
  - Tax-advantage (lessee can deduct depreciation and interest expense)
  - Shown on Lessee b/s
  - Long-term (noncancelable)
  - ↑ leverage ratio

- Net advantage to leasing (NAL) = PV of leasing - PV of owning

      + → lease
      - → buy

- Depreciation Shield
  - Asset × % ×(1-t)

- Why Lease
  - Maintenance services
  - Risk reductions
    - Project life (< economic life)
    - Residual Value
    - Operating Risk
  - Portfolio risk reduction → lessor bears risks

Example #5:

Spot Market
- American Terms: $\$/foreign$ (Direct for US investors) *in US*
- European Terms: foreign $/\$$ (Direct for foreign investors) *in foreign*

Bid - Ask

Bid - $\$$ to Sell / foreign → Buy Home

Ask - $\$$ to buy / foreign → Sell Home

Bid < Ask

- Spread % $= \dfrac{ask-bid}{ask}$

- Cross Rate   Bid $= \dfrac{Bid}{Ask}$ Ask $= \dfrac{Ask}{Bid}$

Borrow ↑%   Lend ↓% *invest*

Forward - agree on $\$$ for future transaction

Discount - bid > ask   (subtract from spot) ⎫
Premium - bid < ask   (add to spot) ⎭ outright

- ~~Forward Option~~ Swap Rate : $\dfrac{Forward - Spot}{Spot} * \dfrac{360}{\text{# of forward days}}$

Forward Premium

Futures - agree on future transaction (Mark to Market)
Gain/Loss = (Future - Spot) × Size   Buy - Sell

- forward - negotion
- future - mark to market, traded

Arbitrage. Buy low Sell high

Options
Buyers
   In the $\$$ (Buyers)
- Call - right to buy Spot↑Strike. American - exercise @ ~~maturity~~ any date
- Put - right to sell Spot↓Strike • European - exercise @ maturity date

- Covered call - seller of call option owns the corresponding amount (long)

- Spreads - 2 calls/puts (write + Buy)
  - Bull - Buy + write Calls MP strike highest ⎫
  - Bear - Buy + write Puts MP strike lowest ⎭ Max Spread

  Cost = (Received - Paid) × Contract ↘
         Premium
  Max Earnings = (Spread × Contract) - Cost
         Strike

- Futures Option - option gives buyer long/short position on future contract

REFERENCES

1. Jacobs, P. (2013, October 7). 28% of people went to the same college as their spouse. Retrieved from https://www.businessinsider.com/28-people-marry-attended-same-college-2013-10

2. Goriounova, N. A., & Mansvelder, H. V. (2019, January 25). Genes, cells and brain areas of intelligence. Retrieved from https://www.frontiersin.org/articles/10.3389/fnhum.2019.00044/full

3. Essays, UK. (November 2018). Correlations between IQ scores and academic performance psychology essay. Retrieved from https://www.ukessays.com/essays/psychology/correlations-between-iq-scores-and-academic-performance-psychology-essay.php?vref=1

4. Cohut, M. (2018, February 23). What are the health benefits of being social? Retrieved from https://www.medicalnewstoday.com/articles/321019.php#1

5. National Institute of Neurological Disorders and Stroke. (2019, August 13). Brain basics: understanding sleep. Retrieved from https://www.ninds.nih.gov/Disorders/Patient-Caregiver-Education/Understanding-Sleep

6. Rampton, J. (2019, April 16). Time blocking tips top experts and scientists use to increase productivity. Retrieved from https://www.entrepreneur.com/article/332290

7. Walden University. (2019, April 18). How positive self-talk can make you feel better and be more productive. Retrieved from https://www.waldenu.edu/online-bachelors-programs/bs-in-psychology/resource/how-positive-self-talk-can-make-you-feel-better-and-be-more-productive

8. McLeod, S. A. (2019, Oct 24). Social identity theory. Retrieved from https://www.simplypsychology.org/social-identity-theory.html

9. Romero, C. (2018). What we know about belonging from scientific research. Retrieved from https://mindsetscholarsnetwork.org/research_library/what-we-know-about-belonging-from-scientific-research/

10. Hess, A. J. (2019, May 20). Here's how much the average student loan borrower owes when they graduate. Retrieved from http://www.cnbc.com/2019/05/20/how-much-the-average-student-loan-borrower-owes-when-they-graduate.html

11. Staff, N. P. R., & Doubek, J. (2016, April 17). Attention, students: Put your laptops away. Retrieved from http://www.npr.org/2016/04/17/474525392/attention-students-put-your-laptops-away

12. Murray, M., & Gordon, E. (2016, November). Using multiple senses to improve memory. Retrieved from https://wp.unil.ch/discoverunil/2016/11/using-multiple-senses-to-improve-memory/

13. Hopkin, M. (2004, May 31). Link proved between senses and memory. Retrieved from https://www.nature.com/articles/news040524-12

ACKNOWLEDGEMENTS

"It takes a village." The more I progress through life, this saying cannot be more true. The people in your life make a difference and help you reach new heights. Writing a book was more challenging than I thought and more rewarding than I could have ever imagined. None of this would have been possible without some key players in my life. There are so many people who I consider my mentors. Without any of you, my life would be completely different.

I would like to thank my father, Greg Smith. He was the one that gave me the push and the idea to write this book. He shined the light on the message I needed to share. He always focused on how to add value to other people, he instilled that motto into me as well. His book, *Go Speak Like a Pro without Looking Like a Jack@$$*, was a great example to me on how to share knowledge and add value to others.

To my wife, Ashley. She was my number one influencer, backer, and cheerleader. She always keeps the bar high and pushes me to be better in everything I do. She keeps my flame of helping others strong with her own servant attitude. Thank you for the support you gave me from the time we were in college until now.

A special thanks to Ret. LTC Scott Mann and the Rooftop Leadership community. I have been lucky to train under Scott Mann for the last couple years in leadership. This former Green Beret is an expert on human connection and storytelling. He has taught me to be a part of something bigger than myself. To leave tracks. Thank you for your messages you taught me and your mentorship.

All of this would not have been possible without my friends. All of them were a positive influence on me throughout my years growing up. Even though you may not realize it, you set the bar high for me to be better. Constantly pushing me to be better everyday.

Vince Bevaqua and Katy Mumaw, thank you for helping through this process. Their notes and advice helped me tremendously. Both of them are also aspiring authors writing their own books. It is always nice to have someone that is going through the same experiences and myself. Someone who I can relate to and help me along the way was a huge bonus.

Finally, I would like to thank Self Publishing School (SPS) and my coach, Gary Williams. The SPS program made writing, publishing, and marketing my book a lot easier. They made this daunting task achievable and I thank you for your excellent program.

Your Help is Needed!

Thank You For Reading My Book!

I would really appreciate all your feedback and
I love hearing what you have to say.

Every review matters, and it matters a *lot!*

Head over to Amazon or wherever you purchased
this book to leave an honest review for me.

Thank you so much.
– Brad Smith

ABOUT THE AUTHOR

B rad Smith graduated from Youngstown State University in 2015 with a Bachelor of Science in Business Administration with a double major in accounting and finance. He graduated Summa Cum Laude and maintained a 4.0 GPA while being a member of the Youngstown State baseball team throughout his college career. He is currently the 4th generation of family ownership in his family-owned company, Compco Industries. Brad is passionate about human development and aspires to help people achieve greatness.